Best Games

188 Active and Quiet,
Simple and Sophisticated,
Games for Preschoolers through Adults

Linda Jennings
Mary L. Lamp
Jerome Stenberg

McFarland & Company, Inc., Publishers
Jefferson, North Carolina, and London

Library of Congress Cataloging in Publication Data

Jennings, Linda, 1946–
   Best games.

   Bibliography : p.
   Includes index.
   1. Games—Handbooks, manuals, etc. I. Lamp, Mary L.
II. Stenberg, Jerome, 1955–   . III. Title.
GV1201.J46 1985   794   84-43237

ISBN 0-89950-159-1 (pbk.)

Manufactured in the United States of America

McFarland Box 611 Jefferson NC 28640

Table of Contents

Introduction

THIS BOOK CONTAINS 188 selected games -- games for everyone, from those who hate to play games to those who love to play them. There are games for preschoolers, school-age youngsters, teens and adults; games for living rooms; games for spacious backyards; games for large, active groups; games for small groups that want a quiet time.

From simple to sophisticated, here are games you can count on for a good time at parties, to entertain youngsters, to pep up a gathering of long-time friends, to use to get better acquainted with new friends. Best of all, the games have been precisely indexed and put in a format that shows you quickly and easily what you need to know to select the right game for your group.

Key

LEVEL OF ACTIVITY: This describes the amount of physical activity associated with the game.

1. Little activity
2. Moderate activity
3. Much activity

WHO:
A. Preschool - Age 7
B. Ages 8 - 12
C. Teen-age
D. Adult

Master Index

Title	Activity Level	Age Level	Players	WHERE? Indoor	Out
Adverbs	1	D	4 +	I	
Advertisements	1	CD	5 +	I	O
Affinities	1	CD	4 +	I	
Air, Land, Water	1	B C	5 + ⚡	I	O
Airplane Race	2	AB C	6 +	I	O
Alphabet Adjectives	1	B CD	4 +	I	
Amoeba	3	B CD	6 +		O
Are You Out There?	2	B CD	8 + ⚔	I	O
Arise	2	B C	2 +	I	O
Arise for Two	2	B C	6 + ⚔	I	O
Artists	2	B CD	4 +	I	
At Sea	3	B CD	8 + ⚔	I	O
Backward Bowling	2	B C	2 +		O
Balancing the Books	2	B C	3 +	I	
Ball Roll	2	A	3 +	I	O
Balloon Ball	3	B C	8 + ⚔	I	
Balloon Break	3	B CD	4 +	I	O
Balloon Relay	3	B CD	6 +	I	O
Balloon Volleyball	3	B CD	4 +		O
Barnyard Buddy	2	B C	8 + ⚡	I	O
Bean Transfer	2	B C	6 +	I	
Bell Bluff	2	B CD	6 +	I	
Bellringer	2	AB	4 +		O
Bird, Beast or Fish	1	B CD	6 +	I	O
Birds Fly	2	AB	3 +	I	O
Blind Man's Bluff	2	B CD	6 +	I	O
Bottle Answer	1	B CD	5 +	I	
Bounce	2	B C	2 +	I	O
Button Sort	2	B C	3 +	I	
Call Ball	3	B C	4 +		O
Call Out Ball	3	B C	6 +		O
Captain, May I?	2	B	5 +	I	O
Capture	2	B C	8 + ⚔	I	O
Capture the Flag	3	B	6 +	I	O
Card Toss	1	B C	4 +	I	
Cat and Dog	2	B CD	2 +	I	
Cat and Mice	3	B	8 + ⚔		O
Cat and Mouse	3	B C	10 + ⚡	I	O
Catch Ball	3	B C	10 + ⚔		O
Categories	1	CD	3 +	I	
Caterpillar Race	3	B C	8 + ⚔		O

5

Title	Activity Level	Age Level	Players	WHERE? Indoor	Out
Cause and Effect	1	B C D	3 +	I	
Celebrities	2	B C	4 +	I	
Chain Tag	3	A B C	4 +		O
Chain Words	2	B C D	5 +	I	O
Change Partners	2	B C	7 +	I	O
Charley Over the Water	3	A B	6 +	I	O
Chin Game	2	C D	8 +	I	O
Circle Race	3	A B C	3 +		O
Circle Tug of War	3	B C D	8 +		O
Coat and Hat Relay	3	B C	8 +		O
Coin Collector	1	B C D	4 +	I	
Coin Drop	1	A B	2 +	I	
Colors	1	A	2 +	I	
Compliments	1	B C D	4 +	I	
Contrary Actions	2	B C D	4 +	I	O
Cooperative Art	2	A B C	4 +	I	
Cooperative Tale	1	B C D	4 +	I	O
Dark Draw	2	B	3 +	I	
Dot Art	2	B C D	3 +	I	
Double Words	1	D	2 +	I	
Dramatic Poetry	1	B C D	4 +	I	
Draw the Tail on the Donkey	2	B C D	3 +	I	
Drop the Handkerchief	3	A B C	6 +	I	O
Duck, Duck, Gray Duck	3	A B	4 +	I	O
Duck Walk	3	B	2 +	I	O
Duet	2	B C D	6 +	I	O
Egg Race	2	B C D	4 +	I	O
Fabric Match	1	A B	2 +	I	O
Famous Names	1	B C D	4 +	I	
Farmer in the Dell	2	A B	8 +	I	O
Feather Float	3	B C D	8 +	I	O
Find It	2	B C D	6 +	I	
Fire Chief	3	B C	13 +		O
Fish	3	B C D	4 +	I	O
Fishing for Paper Clips	2	A B C	2 +	I	
Follow the Leader	3	A B C D	4 +	I	O
Food for Thought	1	A B	2 +	I	O
Forbidden Word	1	B C D	4 +	I	
Glove Relay	2	B C D	6 +	I	
Go Find the Swatter	3	B	5 +	I	O
Good Morning!	2	B C	6 +	I	O
Grandmother's Trunk	1	B C D	3 +	I	O
Group Hide and Seek	2	A B	4 +	I	O
Group Musical Chairs	3	A B	4 +	I	O
Groups	2	B C	10 +	I	O
Guess Ball	2	B C	4 +	I	O
Guess the Leader	2	B C D	6 +	I	
Guessing Contest	1	B C D	4 +	I	O
Ha, Ha, Ha	1	B C D	5 +	I	O

Title	Activity Level	Age Level	Players	WHERE? Indoor	Out
Hangman	1	B C D	2 +	I	
Hat Exchange	2	B C D	6 +	I	
Have You Seen My Friend?	3	B C	6 +	I	O
Hide and Seek	2	A B	4 +	I	O
Holiday	1	B C	6 +	I	
Hot and Cold	2	A B	2 +	I	
Hot Money	2	A B C	8 + ✹	I	O
Hot Potato	2	B C D	5 +	I	O
How Do You Like Your Neighbors?	2	B C D	5 +	I	O
Howdy, Neighbor	2	B C D	10 + ✹		O
Hunt the Thimble	2	B C D	4 +	I	
Hunters and Hunted	3	B C	8 +	I	O
I Don't Like...	1	C D	4 +	I	
I Love My Love	1	C D	4 +	I	
In Plain Sight	2	C D	4 +	I	
In This House	1	B C	3 +	I	
Indoor Football	2	A B C D	4 +	I	
Indoor Scavenger Hunt	1	D	6 +	I	
Kangaroo Race	3	B C	3 +	I	O
Keep Away	3	B C	3 +		O
Kerchief Grab	3	B C	6 +	I	
Kerchief Relay	3	B	10 + ✹	I	O
Laughing	2	A B C D	5 +	I	O
Letter Trace	1	A B	2 +	I	O
Lifesaver Relay	2	B C D	8 + ✹	I	
London Bridge	2	A	4 +	I	O
Look and Remember	1	B C	3 +	I	O
Making Squares	1	B C D	2 +	I	
Marble Golf	2	B C	3 +		O
Mrs. O'Leary's Cow	1	B C D	3 +	I	
Murder	2	C D	6 +	I	
Musical Chairs	3	B C D	5 +	I	
Nursery Rhyme	1	B	2 +	I	
Packing for a Trip	1	B C D	6 +	I	O
Pair Tag	3	B C	6 +		O
Paper, Scissors, Stone	2	B C	2 +	I	O
Pass It On	2	A B C	6 +	I	O
Pass the Prize	2	A B	5 +	I	O
Peanut Drop	1	B C D	3 +	I	
Peanut Relay	2	B C D	6 +	I	O
People Puzzle	2	B C D	6 +	I	O
Pickle in the Middle	3	B	3	I	O
Picture This	2	C D	6 +	I	
Pin the Tail on the Donkey	2	A B C D	3 +	I	
Pinch Me	3	B C D	10 + ✹	I	
Pitch and Catch	3	B	8 + ✹		O
Plate Sailing	2	B C D	2 +	I	O
Pom Pom Pullaway	3	A B	3 +		O

7

Title	Activity Level	Age Level	Players	Indoor	Out
Poor Pussy	2	A B C	6 +	I	O
Posing	2	B C D	6 +	I	O
Progressive Story	1	C D	8 +	I	
Props	1	D	8 +	I	
Puppy Race	3	A B	4 +		O
Pussy Wants a Corner	2	B	5 +	I	
Red Rover	3	B C D	8 +		O
Ribbon Cutting	2	B C D	4 +	I	
Ring-Around-the-Rosy	2	A	3 +	I	O
Ring on a String	2	B C D	6 +	I	O
Ring Relay	2	B C D	8 +	I	
Sardines	2	B C D	4 +	I	
Scavenger Hunt	1	B C D	6 +		O
Sculptor	2	B C D	5 +	I	O
Sensible Sentence	1	B C D	2 +	I	
Shadow Tag	3	B C	4 +		O
Share the Treat	1	B C D	4 +	I	O
Shoe Match	2	A	5 +	I	
Shoe Put	3	B C D	3 +		O
Shoe Scramble	3	A	3 +	I	O
Simon Says	3	A B C	4 +	I	O
Sing Along	2	B C D	10 +	I	O
Sounds Like	1	B C D	3 +	I	
Spellout	1	B C	6 +	I	
Spider Web	2	A B	2 +	I	O
Squat Tag	3	A B C	4 +		O
Squirrel in a Tree	3	B C D	8 +	I	O
Statues	2	B C D	4 +	I	O
String Relay	2	B C	6 +	I	O
Suitcase Relay	3	B C D	8 +	I	O
Tag	3	A B	3 +		O
"10"	2	B C D	10 +	I	O
Things	1	C D	4 +	I	
Tick Tock	2	B	4 +	I	
Toy Shop	2	A B	5 +	I	O
Treasure Hunt	2	B C D	6 +	I	O
Twenty Questions	1	B C D	5 +	I	
Umbrella Ball	2	B C D	2 +	I	
Up, Jenkins!	2	B C D	6 +	I	O
Walking Game	2	B C D	2 +		O
Wastebasket Ball	1	B C D	3 +	I	
What Am I Doing?	2	C D	8 +	I	
What Animal Am I?	2	A B	4 +	I	
What Word?	1	B C D	3 +	I	
Where Am I?	1	B C D	4 +	I	
Who Am I?	2	C D	4 +	I	O
Word Match I	2	B C D	6 +	I	O
Word Match II	2	C D	10 +	I	O
Yes and No	1	B C D	3 +	I	O
You've Got a...	1	B C D	3 +	I	

The Games

ADVERBS

Preparation: None.

How: One player is chosen to be "It" and leaves the room. The other players choose an adverb that can be demonstrated in pantomime. "It" is called back into the room and asks individual players to perform an action in the manner of the adverb. When "It" correctly guesses the adverb, "It" also names the player who gave the most helpful clue. That person becomes the next "It."

Level of Activity: 1

Who: D

4 or more players

Location: indoor

ADVERTISEMENTS

Preparation: Cut out product advertisements from magazines, one for each player. Pins, paper and pencils for all players.

How: Pin an advertisement to the back of each player. Each player asks questions to determine what product is represented on his or her back. After a specified time, the players try to guess the product represented.

Level of Activity: 1

Who: C,D

5 or more players

Location: indoor, outdoor

AFFINITIES

Preparation: Pencils and paper for each player.

How: The game may be played by individuals or pairs of players. The object is to list as many paired things as possible in a set time. A prize is given for the longest list. Examples should be given before the game starts, such as "Salt and Pepper," "Man and Wife," etc.

Level of Activity: 1

Who: C,D

4 or more players

Location: indoor

AIR, LAND, WATER

Preparation: None.

How: Players sit in a circle with "It" in the center. "It" points to another player, calls "Air," "Land," or "Water," and quickly counts to 10. The player selected must name a dweller of the environment called before "It" reaches "10." If unsuccessful, the player becomes "It." Players may not repeat answers.

Level of Activity: 1

Who: B,C

5 or more players

Location: indoor, outdoor

AIRPLANE RACE

Preparation: One cone-shaped paper cup with a hole cut in the bottom and 15 feet of string or twine for each team. Pass the string through the hole in the cup.

How: Players are divided into teams of three. Two players on each team hold either end of the twine and line up side-by-side with the other teams. The third member of each team stands at one end of the twine with the paper cup and, at a given signal, blows into the cup to move it the length of the twine. The first team to get the cup moved the length of the twine wins the game.

Level of Activity: 2

Who: A,B,C

6 or more players

Location: indoor, outdoor

ALPHABET ADJECTIVES

Preparation: None.

How: The first player makes up a sentence containing an adjective beginning with the letter "A." The next player repeats the sentence but substitutes an adjective beginning with "B"; each of the following players substitutes an appropriate adjective beginning with "C," "D," etc. Adjectives can be used only once. Any player who cannot take a turn drops out of the game. The last player in the game is the winner.

Level of Activity: 1

Who: B,C,D

4 or more players

Location: indoor

AMOEBA

Preparation: Two ropes long enough to tie around players.

How: Players divide into two teams. Team members bunch up as closely as possible and hold their hands up in the air while someone ties a rope around the entire team at the waist level. At a signal, the teams race to a goal and back.

Level of Activity: 3

Who: B,C,D

6 or more players

Location: outdoor

ARE YOU OUT THERE?

Preparation: Long mailing tube; blindfold; radio, record player or other source of music.

How: Players form a circle. "It" is blindfolded and stands in the center with the mailing tube. Music is played, and the circle moves around "It." When the music stops, players stop, and "It" points the mailing tube toward the circle and asks "Are you out there?" The player pointed out must take hold of the mailing tube and answer "Yes," but with a disguised voice. If "It" guesses correctly, the player and "It" change places.

Level of Activity: 2

Who: B,C,D

8 or more players

Location: indoor, outdoor

ARISE

Preparation: None.

How: Players lie flat on their backs, arms folded. At the signal, players attempt to rise to sitting position and then to their feet without help from their arms. The first player to stand wins the game.

Level of Activity: 2

Who: B,C

2 or more players

Location: indoor, outdoor

ARISE FOR TWO

Preparation: None.

How: Players form pairs and sit back-to-back on the ground or floor. At the signal, players link arms at the elbows and attempt to stand up without unlocking arms. The first pair to stand wins.

Level of Activity: 2

Who: B,C

6 or more players

Location: indoor, outdoor

ARTISTS

Preparation: Cover a wall with wrapping or freezer paper. Crayons and/or markers.

How: Participants draw a mural which becomes the main party decoration.

Level of Activity: 2

Who: B,C,D

4 or more players

Location: indoor

AT SEA

Preparation: None.

How: Each player finds a partner, and each pair secretly selects the name of a fish. Partners are seated next to each other, except that there are two fewer chairs than there are pairs. The pair without chairs are known as "Sharks," and they walk around the room calling the names of fish, such as "Salmon," "Perch," "Bass," etc. Pairs whose names are called get up and follow the "Sharks." When the "Sharks" shout "Sea storm!", all pairs rush for seats. The pair left without seats becomes the "Sharks," and the game continues.

Level of Activity: 3

Who: B,C,D

8 or more players

Location: indoor, outdoor

BACKWARD BOWLING

Preparation: A basketball, soccer ball or similar ball.

How: Standing at the starting line with legs apart, players stoop and use both hands to throw the ball between their legs as far as possible. Distance is measured to where the ball first touches the ground. Players also may compete for the greatest height using the same technique.

Level of Activity: 2

Who: B,C

2 or more players

Location: outdoor

BALANCING THE BOOKS

Preparation: Small books and/or notebooks for all players.

How: Players form a circle. Each places a book/notebook on his or her head, and the circle marches round and round. Players must drop out of the game when the book/notebook falls. The last player in the game wins.

Level of Activity: 2

Who: B,C

3 or more players

Location: indoor

BALL ROLL

Preparation: A volleyball or similar ball.

How: Players sit in a circle with legs spread and roll ball from player to player.

Level of Activity: 2

Who: A

3 or more players

Location: indoor, outdoor

BALLOON BALL

Preparation: Supply of inflated balloons.

How: Players are divided into two equal teams. Each team takes its place at one end of the room. At a given signal, a balloon is tossed up between the two teams. Each team runs forward and tries to bat the balloon to touch the opposite wall; the first team to do so is the winner. If the balloon breaks, another is tossed up in the spot where the break occurred, and the game goes on.

Level of Activity: 3

Who: B,C

8 or more players

Location: indoor

BALLOON BREAK

Preparation: Balloons; string.

How: Tie an inflated balloon to each player's ankle. Players try to push their balloon against another player's in order to break it without breaking their own. The winner is the player whose balloon is not broken.

Level of Activity: 3

Who: B,C,D

4 or more players

Location: indoor, outdoor

BALLOON RELAY

Preparation: One inflated balloon and two smooth sticks for each team.

How: Players line up in equal teams facing a goal line. Players must hold the balloon between the sticks, race to the goal and back, and transfer the balloon and sticks to the next player without touching the balloon. If the balloon is dropped, the player must use the sticks to pick it up. The first team to complete the relay wins.

Level of Activity: 3

Who: B,C,D

6 or more players

Location: indoor, outdoor

BALLOON VOLLEYBALL

Preparation: Twine or rope to tie between two trees or poles. An inflated balloon plus several spares.

How: Tie the twine or rope between the poles or trees about four feet off the ground. Players are divided into two teams. The balloon is given to one team, and at the signal to start they try to bat the balloon across the rope to the other side. Failure to return the balloon results in one point for the other side. The game ends when one team has 10 points.

Level of Activity: 3

Who: B,C,D

4 or more players

Location: outdoor

BARNYARD BUDDY

Preparation: Write the names of farm animals in duplicate on slips of paper.

How: Players draw slips and try to find their partner by moving around imitating the sound made by the animal whose name they have drawn.

Level of Activity: 2

Who: B,C

8 or more players

Location: indoor, outdoor

BEAN TRANSFER

Preparation: Soda straw for each player; two containers with equal numbers of dried beans; two empty containers.

How: Players divide into two groups and form lines facing the containers, one with beans, the other empty. The object of the contest is to transfer the beans to the empty container by sucking on the straw to move one bean at a time. Each player on each team must completely transfer the beans from one container to another. The first team to do so wins.

Level of Activity: 2

Who: B,C

6 or more players

Location: indoor

BELL BLUFF

Preparation: Sufficient number of blindfolds for all but one player. One small bell.

How: This is a variation of BLIND MAN'S BLUFF in which all players but one are blindfolded. The player without the blindfold carries the bell, which is rung periodically. The blindfolded players try to catch the player without the blindfold. The first player to do so exchanges places with the bell-ringer, and the game goes on.

Level of Activity: 2

Who: B,C,D

6 or more players

Location: indoor

BELLRINGER

Preparation: One bell on a string or ribbon. One beanbag or lightweight rubber ball.

How: The bell is suspended from a pole or tree limb approximately six feet in the air. A line is marked off at a six- to fifteen-foot distance from the bell. Players take turns trying to ring the bell by tossing the beanbag or ball at it. Each player hitting the bell gets one point. High-scoring player wins. This can either be a timed game, or a top score can be agreed upon in advance.

Level of Activity: 2

Who: A,B

4 or more players

Location: outdoor

BIRD, BEAST OR FISH

Preparation: None.

How: The player designated as "It" stands before the other players, points to one, says "Bird," "Beast," or "Fish," and counts quickly to 10. The player pointed to must give the name of a "bird," "beast" or "fish" not previously mentioned in the game before "It" stops counting. If the player answers correctly, "It" goes on; if the answer is incorrect, the player becomes "It."

Level of Activity: 1

Who: B,C,D

6 or more players

Location: indoor, outdoor

BIRDS FLY

Preparation: None.

How: The leader calls out the name of a bird or animal. If the creature flies, the players make flying motions with their hands. If the creature does not fly, the players remain still. For example, players would flap their arms on "Ducks fly," but not "Horses fly."

Level of Activity: 2

Who: A,B

3 or more players

Location: indoor, outdoor

BLIND MAN'S BLUFF

Preparation: Blindfold.

How: The player who is "It" is blindfolded and goes to the center of a circle formed by the other players. "It" is spun around several times, after which the circle rotates until "It" says to stop. "It" then tries to identify a player by feel in order to cease being "It." Players may exchange pieces of clothing in order to make identification more difficult.

Level of Activity: 2

Who: B,C,D

6 or more players

Location: indoor, outdoor

BOTTLE ANSWER

Preparation: Pop bottle.

How: Players sit in a circle and take turns spinning a bottle on its side in the middle of the circle. Just before spinning, the spinner asks a question, such as "Who is the best athlete in this room?", "Who is the most beautiful?", etc. The bottle "answers" by pointing at a player when it stops spinning.

Level of Activity: 1

Who: B,C,D

5 or more players

Location: indoor

BOUNCE

Preparation: Four marbles for each player; chalk or string.

How: Using the chalk or string, create a circle about one foot in diameter. Each player places two or more marbles in the center of the circle. Each then takes a turn dropping a marble from eye-level height, trying to aim the shooter marble so it knocks marbles out of the circle. The player wins any marbles knocked out of the circle. If none are knocked out, the player adds a marble to the circle. The game ends when no marbles remain in the circle.

Level of Activity: 2

Who: B,C

2 or more players

Location: indoor, outdoor

BUTTON SORT

Preparation: An assortment of buttons, screws, clips, bobby pins, etc., divided into two equal piles; two blindfolds.

How: Two players are blindfolded at one time and race each other to see who can be the first to correctly sort the pile of items into smaller piles of like items. All other players challenge the winner in round-robin fashion. The winner of the most matches is the champion.

Level of Activity: 2

Who: B,C

3 or more players

Location: indoor

CALL BALL

Preparation: One tennis ball; a blank wall or high solid fence against which the ball can be bounced.

How: One player is given the tennis ball. That player throws the ball against the wall or fence and calls out another player's name. If the player whose name is called can catch the ball, that player throws the ball and calls yet another player's name. If the first player whose name is called misses the ball, the original pitcher continues to throw and call names until someone catches the ball.

Level of Activity: 3

Who: B,C

4 or more players

Location: outdoor

CALL OUT BALL

Preparation: Large beach ball.

How: One player is selected as "It." "It" stands in a circle of other players and throws the ball into the air while calling out the name of one of the players. The player then runs into the circle and tries to catch the ball. If the player catches the ball, the player becomes "It"; if the player fails to catch the ball, the game continues with the same "It."

Level of Activity: 3

Who: B,C

6 or more players

Location: outdoor

CAPTAIN, MAY I?

Preparation: None.

How: One player is selected as Captain and stands at one end of the playing space. The other players face the Captain, who instructs each player in turn to take a certain number of steps; e.g., "John, take two giant steps," "Linda, take three baby steps" (other possibilities are hops and jumps). Before carrying out the instructions, the player must ask

"Captain, may I?" The Captain can either give or deny permission. The first player to reach and tag the Captain becomes the next Captain.

Level of Activity: 2

Who: B

5 or more players

Location: indoor, outdoor

C A P T U R E

Preparation: Blindfold; chair.

How: Players count off consecutively and form a circle. One player is selected as "It." "It" is blindfolded and sits on a chair in the center of the circle. "It" calls the number of a player, stands and moves two feet from the chair. The player whose number is called attempts to reach the chair without being tagged by "It." If "It" tags the player, the player becomes "It," and the old "It" joins the circle.

Level of Activity: 2

Who: B,C

8 or more players

Location: spacious indoor
area, outdoor

C A P T U R E   T H E   F L A G

Preparation: A stick with a white handkerchief tied to one end.

How: Players divide into two teams. One team has the stick. The teams line up and face each other; the Catchers start the game by saying "We've come to capture the flag." At that point, the team with the stick runs off, passing the stick from one to another and trying to hide it. Once a Catcher has a hold of the stick, however, the stick must be given up.   Then the first team pursues the Catchers, trying to recapture the stick.   The game may be continued as long as desired.

Level of Activity: 3

Who: B

6 or more players

Location: spacious indoor
area, outdoor

CARD TOSS

Preparation: Two decks of cards with different backs; a bowl or wastebasket.

How: Players are divided into two equal teams.   The teams sit in semicircles around the bowl or waste-basket.   The two teams each divide one pack of cards equally among the members.   One member of each team alternately tries to toss one card into the container.   When all the cards have been tossed, those inside the container are counted, and the team with more cards in the container wins the game.

Level of Activity: 1

Who: B,C

4 or more players

Location: indoor

CAT AND DOG

Preparation: Dining room, ping-pong or large kitchen table; two blindfolds; timer.

How: Two players, one representing the Dog and the other the Cat, are blindfolded and stationed at opposite ends of the table with both hands touching the table. Neither knows where the other is or the direction of pursuit. At the signal, the Dog tries to catch the Cat, and the Cat, listening intently, tries to evade the Dog. If the Dog is unable to touch the Cat within a period of two minutes, the Cat wins; otherwise, the Dog is the winner.

Level of Activity: 2

Who: B,C,D

2 or more players

Location: indoor

CAT AND MICE

Preparation: Enough paper plates to serve as markers or mouse holes.

How: Markers are laid out at random about eight to ten feet apart. One player is selected to be the Cat. The remaining players are Mice, and all but one stand on plates which represent mouse holes. At the word "Go," the Cat proceeds to chase the Mouse without a hole. When the chased Mouse tires, another Mouse assumes the role of the Mouse without a hole. When the Cat catches a Mouse, they trade places, and the game goes on.

Level of Activity: 3

Who: B

8 or more players

Location: outdoor

CAT AND MOUSE

Preparation: None.

How: Two players are chosen to be the Cat and the Mouse. The other players join hands and form a circle with the Mouse inside and the Cat outside the circle. The Cat tries to catch the Mouse, and the other players try to protect the Mouse. If the Cat succeeds in catching the Mouse, two other players are selected to be Cat and Mouse, and the game goes on.

Level of Activity: 3

Who: B,C

10 or more players

Location: indoor, outdoor

CATCH BALL

Preparation: One large inflated ball.

How: One player stands inside a circle formed by the other players. The players forming the circle pass the ball at random among themselves. If the ball is intercepted or knocked from a player's hands, the player in the center of the circle changes places with the last player to touch the ball before the interception.

Level of Activity: 3

Who: B,C

10 or more players

Location: outdoor

CATEGORIES

Preparation: Paper and pencils for each player; timer.

How: Choose a five-letter word and write the word perpendicularly at the far left-hand side of the paper. Next, each player suggests a category, such as sports, movie stars, TV stars, etc. and writes each category horizontally across the top of the page. At the signal, each player fills in underneath the categories the names of persons or things beginning with the letter found in the left-hand column. After five minutes, everyone stops writing, and scoring begins. Score one point for each player who did <u>not</u> write the same answer as any other player. Highest-scoring player wins the game.

Level of Activity: 1

Who: C,D

3 or more players

Location: indoor

CATERPILLAR RACE

Preparation: Establish a starting line and, 40 to 60 feet away, a finish line.

How: Players are divided into teams of four to six players each. Each team lines up, one player behind the other. At a signal, the teams run toward the finish line, still maintaining their lineup. The team that maintains its line and finishes first is the winner.

Level of Activity: 3

Who: B,C

8 or more players

Location: outdoor

CAUSE AND EFFECT

Preparation: None.

How: The first player describes any event in simplest terms, such as "The roast burned." The second player must give a reason, such as ". . . Because it was in the oven too long." The third player must then state a result, such as ". . . And everyone had burnt meat." The next player starts with a new statement, and so on.

Level of Activity: 1

Who: B,C,D

3 or more players

Location: indoor

CELEBRITIES

Preparation: Prepare a list of names for possible interviews, such as characters from books, TV stars, musicians, athletes, etc.

How: One player selects and plays the role of the "celebrity" to be interviewed. The other players are the interviewers.

Level of Activity: 2

Who: B,C

4 or more players

Location: indoor

CHAIN TAG

Preparation: None.

How: One player is selected as "It." "It" chases the other players until one individual is caught. That player joins hands with "It," and they continue to chase the other players. As each additional player is tagged, they join onto the chain of chasers. The game continues until one player is left uncaught. This player becomes "It" for the next game.

Level of Activity: 3

Who: A,B,C

4 or more players

Location: outdoor

CHAIN WORDS

Preparation: Beanbag.

How: The game starts with the player with the beanbag saying a word and tossing the beanbag to another player. Each player who gets the beanbag must say a word that logically follows the immediately previous word. For example, "white" may be followed by "snow," followed by "storm," followed by "coat," etc. The player who cannot think of an appropriate word receives a point. The player with the least number of points is the winner.

Level of Activity: 2

Who: B,C,D

5 or more players

Location: indoor, outdoor

CHANGE PARTNERS

Preparation: None.

How: All players except one pair up and stand throughout the playing area. The player without a partner gives commands for the others to follow, such as "Knee to knee," "Hands on hip," "Back to back," "Join right hands." Eventually the single player says "Change partners," and all players must find new partners. The player who does not get a partner starts the game again.

Level of Activity: 2

Who: B,C

7 or more players

Location: spacious indoor
area, outdoor

CHARLEY OVER THE WATER

Preparation: None.

How: Players form a small circle, with one player in the center as "It." The players march around the circle, singing:

> "Charley over the water,
> Charley over the sea,
> Charley caught a big bird
> But can't catch me!"

When the last word is sung, all stop and try to place a hand on the floor before "It" can tag them. If tagged, that player becomes "It."

Level of Activity: 3

Who: A,B

6 or more players

Location: spacious indoor
area, outdoor

CHIN GAME

Preparation: Two identical pieces of fruit, such as apples, grapefruit or oranges.

How: Players divide into two teams and form a line. The first person in each line places the fruit under the chin and proceeds to pass the fruit to the next person in line without using hands. The first team to complete the transfer wins.

Level of Activity: 2

Who: C,D

8 or more players

Location: indoor, outdoor

CIRCLE RACE

Preparation: Mark off a large circle.

How: Players stand facing clockwise with an even distance between each player. At the word "Go," players all run, each trying to pass and tag the runner ahead. If a player is passed and tagged, that player drops out of the game. The last player untagged wins the game.

Level of Activity: 3

Who: A,B,C

3 or more players

Location: outdoor

CIRCLE TUG OF WAR

Preparation: A long, sturdy rope with the ends tied together.

How: Players form a circle, holding the rope. A line is drawn across the circle. Players on each side of the line form the two teams. At a signal, the teams pull. The first team to pull the other team over the line wins the contest.

Level of Activity: 3

Who: B,C,D

8 or more players

Location: outdoor

COAT AND HAT RELAY

Preparation: Establish a starting line and, 40 to 60 feet away, a turning line. An old hat and coat for each team.

How: Players form two teams of four to six players or more. The first player on each team is given a hat and coat. At a signal, the player runs toward the turning line, putting on the coat and hat while running. On the way back, the hat and coat are removed and passed to the next player at the starting line. The first team to complete the race is the winner.

Level of Activity: 3

Who: B,C

8 or more players

Location: outdoor

COIN COLLECTOR

Preparation: Ten assorted coins for each player; a blindfold for each player.

How: Players are seated at a table and blindfolded. Ten coins are spread out in front of each player. At the word "Go," each player tries to sort the coins into piles by denominations. The first player who feels that the correct arrangement has been made shouts "Stop!" All sorting stops while the arrangement is checked. If correct, the player is declared the winner; if it is not correct, the game goes on until a winner is declared.

Level of Activity: 1

Who: B,C,D

4 or more players

Location: indoor

COIN DROP

Preparation: Large wide-mouth container full of water with a small jar or glass sunk in the middle; five small coins for each player; a few additional coins for play-offs.

How: The container is set on the floor, and one at a time the players try to drop their coins from a standing position into the sunken jar or glass. Each player's score is kept, and a tie for first is decided with a sudden death play-off. The winner keeps the coins outside the small jar or glass; the runner-up gets to keep the coins in the small jar or glass.

Level of Activity: 1

Who: A,B

2 or more players

Location: indoor

COLORS

Preparation: None.

How: One player is selected to start the game. The player says "I am thinking of something that is in this room that is (names the color of the object)." The rest of the players try to guess the correct object. The first player to guess correctly becomes the new selector of the object to be guessed.

Level of Activity: 1

Who: A

2 or more players

Location: indoor

COMPLIMENTS

Preparation: Paper and pencil.

How: One player leaves the room. Each of the remaining players writes a complimentary remark about the player. The player returns to the room when all the compliments have been written. A player reads the complimentary remarks, and the complimented person must try to guess who made each remark. The first player whose remark is identified becomes the next person to leave the room. If no correct guess is made, the complimented player may select the next person to leave the room.

Level of Activity: 1

Who: B,C,D

4 or more players

Location: indoor

CONTRARY ACTIONS

Preparation: One square scarf or towel.

How: Players form a circle, and each takes hold of the scarf or towel. One player acts as a leader and says "Let go" or "Hold tight." The other players then must do just the opposite. Players who do not perform the opposite action drop out of the game until only one individual is left.

Level of Activity: 2

Who: B,C,D

4 or more players

Location: indoor, outdoor

COOPERATIVE ART

Preparation: Paper and pencils, markers or crayons for all players.

How: Each player draws a head and neck on the top third of a piece of paper, not showing anyone what has been drawn. Each paper is folded over and passed to the next player, who draws the body or trunk. The paper is again folded over and passed to the next player, who draws the legs and feet. The works of art are then unfolded and displayed.

Level of Activity: 2

Who: A,B,C

4 or more players

Location: indoor

COOPERATIVE TALE

Preparation: None.

How: Players sit in a circle. One player starts a story but stops after one to two sentences. The next player adds one or two sentences, as do each of the other players. The object is to keep the story going for either a selected time or number of rounds of the circle.

Level of Activity: 1

Who: B,C,D

4 or more players

Location: indoor, outdoor

DARK DRAW

Preparation: Paper and pencils for all players; dark room.

How: All players receive a sheet of paper and pencil. The lights are turned off, and players have five minutes to draw anything they want. The players may judge who drew the best picture.

Level of Activity: 2

Who: B

3 or more players

Location: indoor

DOT ART

Preparation: Paper (8½" X 11") and pencils for all players.

How: Each player places 20 dots on the paper and passes the paper to the player on the right. Each player then draws a picture by connecting all the dots on the page in any manner desired.

Level of Activity: 2

Who: B,C,D

3 or more players

Location: indoor

DOUBLE WORDS

Preparation: None.

How: The first player mentions a double word (e.g., "shotgun"). The next player takes the second word and makes it the first word of another pair of double words (e.g., "gun dog"). The game goes on until two players in a row cannot supply the next double word.

Level of Activity: 1

Who: D

2 or more players

Location: indoor

DRAMATIC POETRY

Preparation: None.

How: Players take turns reciting Mother Goose or other familiar rhymes dramatically, with much gesturing. For example, players may present "Jack and Jill" as a tragedy, melodrama or comedy.

Level of Activity: 1

Who: B,C,D

4 or more players

Location: indoor

DRAW THE TAIL ON THE DONKEY

Preparation: Draw or cut out a large picture of a donkey, pig or any object with a part missing. Color crayons--one color for each player.

How: Played like PIN THE TAIL ON . . . games, each player is in turn blindfolded and tries to mark the missing part on the appropriate spot. The individual coming the closest wins the game.

Level of Activity: 2

Who: B,C,D

3 or more players

Location: indoor

DROP THE HANDKERCHIEF

Preparation: Handkerchief.

How: Players form a circle. "It" circles the group and drops the handkerchief behind one of the players, who chases "It" around the circle. If "It" reaches the vacant space before being tagged, the chaser becomes "It."

Level of Activity: 3

Who: A,B,C

6 or more players

Location: spacious indoor
   area, outdoor

DUCK, DUCK, GRAY DUCK

Preparation: None.

How: Players sit on the floor or ground facing each other
   in a circle except for one player who is "It." "It"
   walks behind the seated players, tapping their
   heads and saying, for example, "Duck," "Black
   duck," "Blue duck," "White duck," etc. When "It"
   taps a head and says "Gray duck," the seated player
   jumps up and runs after "It," trying to tag "It"
   before "It" reaches the vacated spot. If unsuccessful, "Gray duck" becomes the new "It."

Level of Activity: 3

Who: A,B

4 or more players

Location: spacious indoor
   area, outdoor

DUCK WALK

Preparation: Establish a starting line and finish line.

How: Players stoop and grasp ankles with their hands.
   At a signal, the players proceed to race to the
   finish line. The first one crossing the line wins.

Level of Activity: 3

Who: B

2 or more players

Location: spacious indoor
    area, outdoor

DUET

Preparation: Make a list of familiar song titles in duplicate on slips of paper.

How: Each player draws the name of a song and proceeds to hum or whistle it in order to try to find the other player who is humming or whistling the same song.

Level of Activity: 2

Who: B,C,D

6 or more players

Location: indoor, outdoor

EGG RACE

Preparation: One large spoon per player; one hard-boiled egg or small ball per player. Mark start and finish lines.

How: At the word "Go!", players must carry an egg or ball in a spoon from the starting line across the finish line without dropping it. The first player to do this wins the game.

Level of Activity: 2

Who: B,C,D

4 or more players

Location: indoor, outdoor

FABRIC MATCH

Preparation: Swatches of different fabrics, such as felt, velvet, corduroy, etc. (two of each kind); a bag.

39

How: Each player feels the fabrics in the bag and by using only the sense of touch tries to select the duplicate swatches. More fabrics may be used for older children to make the game more difficult.

Level of Activity: 1

Who: A,B

2 or more players

Location: indoor, outdoor

FAMOUS NAMES

Preparation: Paper and pencil for each player; timer.

How: A letter is announced, and at the signal each player writes down famous people whose names begin with the letter. First names may be used. Characters in history, fiction and the Bible, politicians, athletes, movie stars, entertainers, etc., may be listed. The player with the most names at the end of the time period wins. The game also may be played by limiting correct answers to a certain classification, such as athletes, historic names, etc.

Level of Activity: 1

Who: B,C,D

4 or more players

Location: indoor

FARMER IN THE DELL

Preparation: None.

How: Players form a circle, join hands and walk around another player who is the "Farmer." Players sing:

Verse 1   "The Farmer in the dell, the
               Farmer in the dell,

Heigho, the derry-o, the Farmer
in the dell."

Verse 2   "The Farmer takes a Wife, the
Farmer takes a Wife,
Heigho, the derry-o, the Farmer
takes a Wife."

The "Farmer" then chooses a "Wife," who joins the
"Farmer" in the middle of the circle. The game
continues with players selecting the "Child," the
"Nurse," the "Dog," the "Cat," the "Rat," and the
"Cheese" as indicated in verses 3 through 9:

Verse 3   "The Wife takes a Child," etc.
Verse 4   "The Child takes a Nurse," etc.
Verse 5   "The Nurse takes a Dog," etc.
Verse 6   "The Dog takes a Cat," etc.
Verse 7   "The Cat takes a Rat," etc.
Verse 8   "The Rat takes the Cheese," etc.
Verse 9   "The Cheese stands alone," etc.

All stand around the "Cheese" and clap as they sing
the last verse.

Level of Activity: 2

Who: A,B

8 or more players

Location: spacious indoor
area, outdoor

FEATHER FLOAT

Preparation: Twelve feet of heavy string; two sturdy but
light feathers.

How: Peg or tape down the string to create two sides.
Divide the players into two teams. Each team
tries to blow its feather over to the other side
(where it counts one point if it falls to the ground)
while at the same time trying to blow away the
other team's feather. The first team to accumu-

late 10 points wins. Scoring can also be on the basis of time, with the winning team being the one scoring the most points during a timed interval.

Level of Activity: 3

Who: B,C,D

8 or more players

Location: indoor, outdoor

FIND IT

Preparation: A small object to hide. The object can be related to the theme of the party.

How: Players are sent from the room, and the object is hidden with a small part of it remaining in view. Players are called back and told to look for the object but not to say anything when they see it; they are to go to a corner of the room, sit on the floor, and sing any song they choose. After all the players have found it, the first person to have seen the object wins it as a prize.

Level of Activity: 2

Who: B,C,D

6 or more players

Location: indoor

FIRE CHIEF

Preparation: Lay out two goal lines 30 feet apart.

How: One player is the Fire Chief, and the others divide into four groups which stand on a goal line 30 feet away from another goal line. The Fire Chief stands in the middle and calls "Fire! Fire! Station Number (One, Two, Three or Four)!" The group corresponding to the number called runs to the opposite goal line and back to the Fire Chief. The first player to touch the Fire Chief's hand trades places with the Fire Chief for the next game. Everyone runs when the Fire Chief calls "Fire! Fire! General Alarm!"; again, the winner is the first player to touch the Fire Chief's hand.

Level of Activity: 3

Who: B,C

13 or more players

Location: outdoor

FISH

Preparation: Approximately five feet of lightweight string for each player; small objects such as a small stick or spool of thread for each player.

How: Each player attaches the small object ("Fish") to the end of the string and ties the other end of the string at or around the waist. With their "Fish" trailing on the floor, players try to capture another player's Fish by stepping on and breaking the string. At the same time, the players try to avoid having their Fish caught. A player whose Fish is caught must leave the game. The last player with a Fish wins the game.

Level of Activity: 3

Who: B,C,D

4 or more players

Location: indoor, outdoor

FISHING FOR PAPER CLIPS

Preparation: Empty a box of paper clips into a cardboard box with high sides; a magnet on a string.

How: The cardboard box of paper clips is placed in the center of a table. The first player is given the

43

magnet on a string ("Hook") and, without standing up or looking in the box, tries to "Hook" as many paper clips ("Fish") as possible. When the Hook is pulled up, the Fish that remain attached are removed and counted. These Fish are "thrown back" into the box, and the game continues until all have had a chance to play. The player who catches the most Fish wins.

Level of Activity: 2

Who: A,B,C

2 or more players

Location: indoor

FOLLOW THE LEADER

Preparation: None.

How: One player is selected as the leader. The other players form a line behind the leader and imitate the leader's actions. The leader keeps the line in motion, walking, hopping, jumping and making arm motions. This is a good way of moving players from one point to another.

Level of Activity: 3

Who: A,B,C,D

4 or more players

Location: indoor, outdoor

FOOD FOR THOUGHT

Preparation: None.

How: The game begins with a statement such as "I saw a candy bar; I one it." In turn, players reply "I two it," "I three it," "I four it," etc., until one player says "I eight it." Older children may want to use such objects as rocks, dead horses, skunks, etc., but perhaps it is best to use more desirable objects with younger children.

Level of Activity: 1

Who: A,B

2 or more players

Location: indoor, outdoor

FORBIDDEN WORD

Preparation: None.

How: One player is selected as "It," and that player leaves the room. The other players agree on a "forbidden" word, and "It" is called back into the room, where the other players carry on a conversation and question "It" in an effort to make "It" use the forbidden word. (One player keeps count of the number of times the word is used.) Meanwhile, "It" tries to guess what the forbidden word is; if "It" guesses correctly, another player is chosen as "It," and the game goes on until all players have had a turn. Lowest score wins the game.

Level of Activity: 1

Who: B,C,D

4 or more players

Location: indoor

GLOVE RELAY

Preparation: Two large purses; two pairs of gloves; a stick of gum for each player; two small paper bags. Divide the gum equally and put into paper bags; a bag of gum goes in each purse.

How: Players divide into two equal teams. While wearing the gloves, each player must open the purse and take a piece of gum from the paper bag, refold the bag, place it in the purse, close the purse, and unwrap and chew the gum. Finally, the player whistles before passing the gloves and purse to the next teammate. The first team to complete the relay wins.

Level of Activity: 2

Who: B,C,D

6 or more players

Location: indoor

GO FIND THE SWATTER

Preparation: A knotted towel.

How: Set aside a small area as goal. One player is "It." While the other players hide their eyes and count together to 50, "It" hides the towel swatter. At the end of the count, the players begin the hunt for the swatter. The finder swats as many players as possible before they can reach the goal and safety. The finder becomes "It" for the next round.

Level of Activity: 3

Who: B

5 or more players

Location: indoor, outdoor

GOOD MORNING!

Preparation: None.

How: Players sit or stand in a group. One player is the voice detective and turns away from the group. The leader of the group points to a player, who says "Good morning, _____," using the detective's first name. The detective replies "Good morning, _____," naming the player who has spoken. If incorrect, the detective may continue guessing (up to five times). If correct, the detective changes places with the player whose voice was recognized. Players may wish to disguise their voices after playing for a while.

Level of Activity: 2

Who: B,C

6 or more players

Location: indoor, outdoor

GRANDMOTHER'S TRUNK

Preparation: None.

How: Decide the order in which players will take their turns. The first player thinks of an object (a hot dog, for example) and starts the game by saying "I put a hot dog in Grandmother's trunk." The next player repeats the statement and adds an item, such as "I put a hot dog and green worms in Grand-mother's trunk." Each player in turn repeats the list of objects and adds one. When this list gets so long that players can't remember all the objects or the right sequence, the list is started over. A person who misses three times is out, and the last person left in the game is the winner.

Level of Activity: 1

Who: B,C,D

3 or more players

Location: indoor, outdoor

GROUP HIDE AND SEEK

Preparation: Select a place for "It" to stand.

How: One player is selected as "It." While "It" counts out loud to 50 with eyes closed, the other players scatter and hide. When the count is completed,

"It" goes in search of the other players. When "It" locates another player, they join hands and proceed to look for the other players. Each time a player is located, that player joins the group of seekers. The game continues until all players are located.

Level of Activity: 2

Who: A,B

4 or more players

Location: indoor, outdoor

GROUP MUSICAL CHAIRS

Preparation: Line up chairs, one for each player, with every other one reversed. Record player, radio or other source of music.

How: The players march around the chairs in time to the music. When the music is stopped, the players sit down. One chair is then removed, and the game continues with players sharing chairs. The game ends when all players are sharing one chair.

Level of Activity: 3

Who: A,B

4 or more players

Location: indoor, outdoor

GROUPS

Preparation: None.

How: Players scatter throughout the playing area. A leader calls out a number, and all players attempt to form groups of the number called. The player or players left out are eliminated. Players may take turns being the leader.

Level of Activity: 2

Who: B,C

10 or more players

Location: spacious indoor
    area, outdoor

GUESS BALL

Preparation: Tennis ball.

How: One player is selected as "It." The other players sit in a circle. "It" stands in the center of the circle with closed eyes while the players pass the ball in either direction to the player who has been selected to hold it. All of the players pretend to conceal the ball. "It" is then told to look around the circle and guess who has the ball. "It" points directly at the player of choice and says "Throw me the ball." "It" is given three chances to guess who has the ball. If "It" fails to guess correctly, another player is chosen to be "It." If "It" guesses correctly, "It" and the player with the ball change places.

Level of Activity: 2

Who: B,C

4 or more players

Location: indoor, outdoor

GUESS THE LEADER

Preparation: None.

How: One player is selected as "It" and is sent out of the room. The other players arrange themselves in a circle, and a leader is chosen whom the rest of the players will imitate. The player who is "It" returns to the room when the group starts to clap hands. "It" stands in the center of the circle and tries to pick out the leader as the group follows the leader. Actions are changed when "It" is not looking. When the leader is identified, the leader becomes "It," and another leader is chosen.

Level of Activity: 2

Who: B,C,D

6 or more players

Location: indoor

GUESSING CONTEST

Preparation: Prepare several displays, keeping a record of vital statistics, such as a jar of dried beans (number), a ball of twine (inches), a jar of pennies (number), and a jar of jelly beans (number). Paper and pencil for each player.

How: Each player writes a guess for each item. The player with the guess closest to the actual number wins the display item.

Level of Activity: 1

Who: B,C,D

4 or more players

Location: indoor, outdoor

HA, HA, HA

Preparation: None.

How: Players form a circle and sit. The first player says "Ha," the next player says "Ha, ha," the next "Ha, ha, ha," and so on, with each player adding a "ha." The game is to be played with a straight face, and any player who laughs, smiles or fails to say the correct number of "ha"'s is eliminated.

Level of Activity: 1

Who: B,C,D

5 or more players

Location: indoor, outdoor

HANGMAN

Preparation: Pencil and paper.

How: One player thinks of a word and draws a line of dashes to represent the number of letters in the word. A drawing of a gallows is made next to the line of dashes. The other players take turns guessing the letters that make up the word. If correct, the letter is written in the appropriate place; if the letter is wrong, a part of anatomy is added to the gallows. If the gallows figure is completed (one head, one body, two arms, two legs) before the word is guessed, the game is won by the player who started the game.

Level of Activity: 1

Who: B,C,D

2 or more players

Location: indoor

HAT EXCHANGE

Preparation: Enough old hats so that each player has one.

How: One player acts as leader or caller. The other players stand in a circle, each wearing a hat. The caller counts "One," and each player takes hold of a neighbor's hat with the left hand. On the count of "Two," the players transfer the hat in the left hand to their own head. The caller increases the speed of the count as the hats move around the circle.

Level of Activity: 2

Who: B,C,D

6 or more players

Location: indoor

HAVE YOU SEEN MY FRIEND?

Preparation: None.

How: One player is selected as "It." The other players sit in a large circle. "It" stands behind one player and asks "Have you seen my friend?" The player says, "No, what does your friend look like?" "It" then describes the clothing of the "friend" (one of the other players). When the "friend"'s name is guessed, that player jumps up and runs once around the circle, pursued by the first player. (Meanwhile, "It" assumes the first player's place.) If the "friend" can return to the vacant space without being tagged, the new "It" starts again; if tagged, the "friend" goes to the center of the circle and stays there until another "friend" is tagged and comes into the circle as a replacement.

Level of Activity: 3

Who: B,C

6 or more players

Location: indoor, outdoor

HIDE AND SEEK

Preparation: Select a "safety" area where "It" may stand.

How: One player is selected as "It." While keeping eyes closed "It" counts out loud to 50; meanwhile, the other players scatter and hide. When the count is completed, "It" goes in search of the other players. When "It" locates another player, "It" says "I see _____ " and races with the identified player to the "safety" area or goal. Players can also attempt to reach the "safety" without being discovered by

"It." The first player to lose the race to the "safety" becomes "It" in the next game.

Level of Activity: 2

Who: A,B

4 or more players

Location: indoor, outdoor

HOLIDAY

Preparation: None.

How: One player is selected to be "It." The other players form a circle around "It." "It" walks around in the circle and stops in front of one of the players and asks "I am going to Paris (or any other city, state or country). What should I bring back?" "It" then counts to ten, and the player tries to name three items beginning with the first letter of the name of the destination. If the player cannot name three items, "It" and the player change places.

Level of Activity: 1

Who: B,C

6 or more players

Location: indoor

HOT AND COLD

Preparation: Individual treasures (such as gum, suckers, a small toy) for each player. Hide the treasures in one or two rooms.

How: Players try to find a treasure according to signals given by the hider. For example, a player very close to a treasure is "very hot," close is "hot," somewhat close is "warm," and not close is "cold." Players also may be told, for example, that they "are getting hot," to aid them as they move about. Players leave the game when they find a treasure.

Level of Activity: 2

Who: A,B

2 or more players

Location: indoor

HOT MONEY

Preparation: A coin; radio, record player or other source of music.

How: Players form a circle and pass a coin from hand to hand as music is played. When the music stops, the player with the coin must drop out of the game. The winner is the last individual left.

Level of Activity: 2

Who: A,B,C

8 or more players

Location: indoor, outdoor

HOT POTATO

Preparation: A block, handkerchief, ball or similar object; radio, record player or other source of music.

How: Players form a circle, and when the music starts, they pass the object from person to person. The player holding the object when the music stops must drop out of the game. The winner is the last remaining player.

Level of Activity: 2

Who: B,C,D

5 or more players

Location: indoor, outdoor

HOW DO YOU LIKE YOUR NEIGHBORS?

Preparation: Seating for all players except one.

How: Players seat themselves in a circle. One is designated as "It" and stands in the center of the circle. "It" starts the game by asking any other player "How do you like your neighbors?" The player questioned must reply either "Not at all" or "Very much." If the reply is "Not at all," the player is asked which other two players would be preferred, and these named players must then change places with the unwanted neighbors. During the change, "It" tries to sit in one of the empty chairs, leaving one of the four other players as the next "It." If the reply is "Very much," all players must change seats, and "It" attempts to sit in one of the vacated chairs. If "It" succeeds, the player who lost a chair becomes "It."

Level of Activity: 2

Who: B,C,D

5 or more players

Location: indoor, outdoor

HOWDY, NEIGHBOR

Preparation: None.

How: Players choose partners, join hands as pairs and form a circle, with the exception of one pair who walks around the circle counterclockwise. When this pair touches another pair on their joined hands, that pair leaves the circle and walks rapidly in a clockwise direction. The two pairs moving in opposite directions each try to be first to reach the vacated spot. The first pair to reach the vacant spot rejoins the circle; the second pair becomes "It," and the game continues. The game may be played at any pace suitable to the players' age and agility: walking, running, hopping or jumping.

Level of Activity: 2

Who: B,C,D

10 or more players

Location: outdoor

HUNT THE THIMBLE

Preparation: Thimble.

How: One player is selected as "It" and leaves the room. The other players decide where to hide the thimble. "It" is called back into the room, and the other players start to sing a song, singing softly when "It" is far from the thimble and more loudly as "It" gets closer to the thimble. "It" is allowed three minutes after entering the room to find the thimble.

Level of Activity: 2

Who: B,C,D

4 or more players

Location: indoor

HUNTERS AND HUNTED

Preparation: None.

How: Players divide into two equal sides: hunters and hunted. The hunters join hands and try to encircle a member of the hunted team. A player that is encircled is captured and must drop out of the game. When all hunted players have been captured, the teams may change roles.

Level of Activity: 3

Who: B,C

8 or more players

Location: spacious indoor
          area, outdoor

I DON'T LIKE . . .

Preparation: None.

How: One player is selected as "It". Players sit in a circle and "It" announces "I don't like __" (one of the letters of the alphabet). "It" then asks the other players in turn a question which must be answered without using a word containing the forbidden letter. For example:

Forbidden letter: "I don't like 'T'."

> Question: "What did you have for dinner on Thanksgiving?"
>
> Answer: "Cranberries, "Pumpkin pie," or "Dressing" would be acceptable answers; "Turkey" would not.

If a player is unable to answer a question or gives the wrong answer, that player changes places with "It" and selects a new letter.

Level of Activity: 1

Who: C,D

4 or more players

Location: indoor

I LOVE MY LOVE

Preparation: None.

How: One player starts the game by saying "I love my love with an 'A' because he (she) is _____," naming an adjective beginning with an "A." The next player continues the game by saying "I love

my love with a 'B' because he (she) is _____,"
naming an adjective beginning with a "B." The
game continues letter by letter until a player
cannot answer. A point is scored against that
player, and the game starts over with "A."

Level of Activity: 1

Who: C,D

4 or more players

Location: indoor

IN PLAIN SIGHT

Preparation: A tray containing 15 assorted small objects;
pencil and paper for each player.

How: The prepared tray is placed before the players for
them to study. Players are then sent from the
room while the objects from the tray are hidden
around the room, in plain sight but camouflaged so
they are easily overlooked. The players are called
back into the room and given pencil and paper on
the signal to begin the hunt. The goal is to
discover and write down the exact location of all
15 objects. Players may work individually or in
teams of two. The first player or team to complete the list wins.

Level of Activity: 2

Who: C,D

4 or more players

Location: indoor

IN THIS HOUSE

Preparation: None.

How: The beginning player says "I'm thinking of something in this house." Another player asks "In which

room is it?" The first player answers. The questions continue, such as "What color is it?" ("White"), "Is it the white flower pot?" ("No"), etc., until a player guesses the object. That player then becomes the thinker.

Level of Activity: 1

Who: B,C

3 or more players

Location: indoor

INDOOR FOOTBALL

Preparation: Ping-pong ball; table suitable to height of players kneeling.

How: Players are divided into two teams. Each team kneels at either end of a table. A ping-pong ball is dropped in the center of the table, and each team tries to blow the ball off the opposite end of the table. One point is awarded for each "goal," and when an agreed-upon score is reached by one team, that team is declared the winner.

Level of Activity: 2

Who: A,B,C,D

4 or more players

Location: indoor

INDOOR SCAVENGER HUNT

Preparation: Make a list of common objects normally carried; e.g., watch, driver's license, safety pin, 1977 penny.

How: Players are divided into two teams. The leader calls for the objects on the list, one at a time. The first team to produce the object gets one point. When the end of the list is reached, the team with the most points wins the game.

59

Level of Activity: 1

Who: D

6 or more players

Location: indoor

KANGAROO RACE

Preparation: An inflated balloon for each player, extras in case of breakage. Mark start and finish lines about 30 feet apart.

How: Players line up at a starting line and put their balloon between their knees. At the signal, they bend over and hop like a kangaroo to the goal and back. The first player to return to the starting point is the winner. If a balloon breaks, the player must drop out of the race.

Level of Activity: 3

Who: B,C

3 or more players

Location: spacious indoor
area, outdoor

KEEP AWAY

Preparation: Ball or beanbag.

How: One player is selected as "It." The other players form two lines and try to keep the ball or beanbag from "It" by passing the object back and forth. If "It" secures the object, a new "It" is chosen and the game goes on.

Level of Activity: 3

Who: B,C

3 or more players

Location: outdoor

KERCHIEF GRAB

Preparation: Bandana kerchief.

How: Players form a circle. One player stands in the center of the circle and throws the kerchief into the air while calling the name of one of the other players. If the player whose name is called fails to catch the kerchief before it falls to the ground, that player trades places with the one in the center.

Level of Activity: 3

Who: B,C

6 or more players

Location: indoor

KERCHIEF RELAY

Preparation: Two bandana kerchiefs.

How: Players divide into two equal teams and form two circles. One player in each circle is given a kerchief and, at the signal, weaves in and out among the players until reaching the starting point. The player to the right of the first then takes the kerchief and proceeds in a similar fashion. The game continues until all players have carried the kerchief. The circle finishing first wins. Instead of kerchiefs, objects appropriate to the theme of the party may be used.

Level of Activity: 3

Who: B

10 or more players

Location: spacious indoor
        area, outdoor

LAUGHING

Preparation: Handkerchief.

How: All players except one who is "It" form a circle. "It" stands inside the circle and tosses a hand-kerchief into the air. Everyone, including "It," must laugh until the handkerchief touches the floor. Then there must be perfect silence. Anyone laughing after the handkerchief touches the floor becomes "It," and the previous "It" joins the circle.

Level of Activity: 2

Who: A,B,C,D

5 or more players

Location: indoor, outdoor

LETTER TRACE

Preparation: None.

How: A player is selected as "It." "It" slowly traces a letter of the alphabet on another player's back, who tries to guess the letter. If the guess is correct, "It" moves to the next player. If the guess is incorrect, "It" and the player change places, and the game continues.

Level of Activity: 1

Who: A,B

2 or more players

Location: indoor, outdoor

LIFESAVER RELAY

Preparation: Lifesavers; toothpicks for all players.

How: Players divide into two equal teams and form lines. At a signal, the teams pass a Lifesaver from player to player via the toothpick in each player's mouth. If the Lifesaver is dropped before it reaches the end of the line, it must be started over at the beginning of the line. The winning team is the one whose Lifesaver reaches the end of the line first.

Level of Activity: 2

Who: B,C,D

8 or more players

Location: indoor

LONDON BRIDGE

Preparation: None.

How: Two players hold hands and form an arch through which the other players march. All sing:

> "London Bridge is falling down,
> falling down, falling down,
> London Bridge is falling down,
> my fair lady!"

When "my fair lady" is sung, the arch drops around a player. The arch rises and the game continues with the second verse:

> "Build it up with iron bars,
> iron bars, iron bars,
> Build it up with iron bars,
> my fair lady!"

Again, the arch drops on the words "my fair lady." Players then change order, and a new pair forms the arch.

Level of Activity: 2

Who: A

4 or more players

Location: indoor, outdoor

LOOK AND REMEMBER

Preparation: A number of small objects, such as scissors, books, pencils, buttons, utensils, dishes, etc.; a cloth to cover the objects; paper and pencil for all players.

How: Place the objects on a table or a tray. Players may spend five minutes looking at the objects, trying to remember them. Cover the objects and give players paper and pencil to write the names of as many objects as possible. The player who correctly remembers the most objects wins.

Level of Activity: 1

Who: B,C

3 or more players

Location: indoor, outdoor

MAKING SQUARES

Preparation: Paper and pencils.

How: Make five or more rows of dots on a piece of paper (see example). Players take turns connecting any two dots with a straight line, except that diagonals are not allowed. When a player completes a square, that player puts his/her initial in the square. The player with more squares wins.

Example:

Level of Activity: 1
Who: B,C,D

2 players

Location: indoor

MARBLE GOLF

Preparation: A distinctly colored marble for each player. Six or more holes in the ground, each some distance (from one to four feet) from the others.

How: Each player is given a marble and takes turns rolling the marble along the ground from one hole to another. Score is kept, and the player completing the course in the fewest number of turns wins the game.

Level of Activity: 2

Who: B,C

3 or more players

Location: outdoor

MRS. O'LEARY'S COW

Preparation: None.

How: Someone starts the game with "Mrs. O'Leary's cow is an _____ cow," using an adjective starting with "A," such as "active." The next player uses an adjective starting with "B," such as "Mrs. O'Leary's cow is a brown cow." The game continues, using all the letters of the alphabet. As a variation, all the adjectives may be repeated by each player before a new one is added. Any player who cannot supply a word or who fails to repeat the sequence of adjectives drops out of the game.

Level of Activity: 1

Who: B,C,D

3 or more players

Location: indoor

MURDER

Preparation: Prepare slips of paper for each player. Write "Murderer" on one, "Prosecutor" on another, and "Detective" on another; all other slips are blank.

How: Each player draws a slip and does not disclose its contents. The host turns off all lights for one minute. During this time the murderer seizes a player's neck and leaves the scene. The victim screams and falls to the floor. The host turns on the lights. The prosecutor and detective step forward to try to solve the crime by questioning all players, all of whom cooperate except the murderer, who may lie. When prosecutor and detective reach a conclusion, the accused shows the slip of paper. If the slip is blank, the investigation may continue if desired, or the case may be considered another unsolved murder.

Level of Activity: 2

Who: C,D

6 or more players

Location: indoor after dark,
preferably in more
than one room

MUSICAL CHAIRS

Preparation: Line up chairs with every other one reversed, one fewer chair than there are players. Record player, radio or other source of music.

How: The players march around the chairs to music. When the music is stopped, the players sit down. The player without a chair is eliminated, and one chair is removed. The game continues until there is one chair and two players, one of whom is seated.

Level of Activity: 3

Who: B,C,D

5 or more players

Location: spacious indoor area

NURSERY RHYME

Preparation: None.

How: The first player recites the first line of any nursery rhyme. Each following player recites in turn the next line or portion of a line until the whole nursery rhyme is completed. The next player starts with the first line of any other similar poem, and so on.

Level of Activity: 1

Who: B

2 or more players

Location: indoor

PACKING FOR A TRIP

Preparation: None.

How: Players sit in a circle and one starts by saying "I am going on a trip, and I am going to take along my _____ ." The next person repeats this statement and adds an item he wishes to pack. The players take turns repeating the statement and adding to it. Anyone who forgets an item is out. The last person to remember the whole list is the winner.

Level of Activity: 1

Who: B,C,D

6 or more players

Location: indoor, outdoor

PAIR TAG

Preparation: None.

How: Two players are selected from the group. One is "It," and the other acts as "Its Partner". All of the other players try to tag "It," while "It" and "Partner" try to evade the group. The "Partner" cannot be tagged but can tag players, who are then out of the game. If "It" is tagged, the game ends, and a new "It" and "Partner" are chosen.

Level of Activity: 3

Who: B,C

6 or more players

Location: outdoor

PAPER, SCISSORS, STONE

Preparation: None.

How: Players select paper, scissors, or stone and represent the object with their hand. Paper is portrayed by a flat hand, scissors by two extended fingers and stone by a fist. Together the players count to three; on "three" they present their object. The player wins according to:

Stone breaks scissors (Stone wins)
Scissors cut paper (Scissors wins)
Paper covers stone (Paper wins)

Players may elect to play to a certain point total.

Level of Activity: 2

Who: B,C

2 or more players

Location: indoor, outdoor

PASS IT ON

Preparation: Four similar-sized containers. Fill two of the containers with the same number of miscellaneous small items: books, pens, pencils, etc.

How: Players line up in two equal teams. One filled container is placed at the front end of each team and an empty container at the back. At a signal, the first player takes one object at a time out of the front container and passes them down the line to be deposited into the empty container at the back of the line. If an item is dropped, it must be passed back to the head of the line and started again. The first team to transfer all the items wins.

Level of Activity: 2

Who: A,B,C

6 or more players

Location: indoor, outdoor

PASS THE PRIZE

Preparation: Wrap a small prize in a number of layers of wrapping paper, taping or tying each layer as securely as the players can handle easily. Record player, radio or other source of music.

How: Players are seated in a circle. As music is played, the package is passed hand-to-hand. When the music stops, the player holding the package removes a single layer of the wrapping. The music resumes and stops as often as is necessary to get to the last layer of wrapping; the player who unwraps the last layer gets to keep the prize.

Level of Activity: 2

Who: A,B

5 or more players

Location: indoor, outdoor

PEANUT DROP

Preparation: One-quart jar; 15 to 25 peanuts per player; straight-back chair.

How: Players take turns kneeling on a chair and dropping their peanuts one-by-one over the back of the chair into the jar. The player who can drop the most nuts into the jar in two minutes wins the contest.

Level of Activity: 1

Who: B,C,D

3 or more players

Location: indoor

PEANUT RELAY

Preparation: Table knives and a supply of peanuts in the shell; obstacles, which are optional.

How: Players are divided into two or more teams. The first person in each team is given a table knife and a peanut. At the signal to start, the player balances the peanut on the blade of the knife and proceeds to the finish line and back. Each of the players in turn does the same. The team finishing first is the winner. If a peanut is dropped, it must be picked up and rebalanced on the knife. The game can be made more difficult by setting up an obstacle course for each team to follow to the finish line and back.

Level of Activity: 2

Who: B,C,D

6 or more players

Location: indoor, outdoor

PEOPLE PUZZLE

Preparation: None.

How: Players form a circle, except for one player who is "It" and stands outside the circle. "It" turns away from the circle and closes eyes. The circle of players, meanwhile, proceeds to tangle itself up without letting go of hands. This may be done by having players come across the circle and go through an arch formed by two players. In a good tangle, a player has difficulty knowing whose hand is holding whose. "It," when called back, must untangle the snarled-up circle without breaking handholds.

Level of Activity: 2

Who: B,C,D

6 or more players

Location: spacious indoor area, outdoor

PICKLE IN THE MIDDLE

Preparation: Large rubber ball.

How: One player is the "pickle." The other two players stand about 10 feet apart and throw the ball to each other, trying to throw it high enough or fast enough so the "pickle" can't catch it. If a player fails to catch the ball, the "pickle" is free to scramble for it. If the "pickle" gets the ball, the player who threw it and the "pickle" trade places. The game continues as long as desired, as there really is no winner or loser.

Level of Activity: 3

Who: B

3 players

Location: spacious indoor area, outdoor

PICTURE THIS

Preparation: Pad and pencil for each team captain.

How: Players are divided into two teams, or more if there are a large number of players. Each team selects a captain, who is given a pad and pencil. At a signal, the captains come forward and are given a word or phrase. The captains then go back to their teams and draw a picture of the word or phrase, and the other players try to guess the word or phrase from the picture. The first team to guess correctly wins.

Level of Activity: 2

Who: C,D

6 or more players

Location: indoor

PIN THE TAIL ON THE DONKEY

Preparation: Draw a donkey on a large piece of paper and mount it on cardboard, a wall, corkboard, etc. Cut out a drawing of a donkey's tail. Tape or thumbtacks; blindfold.

How: Each player is blindfolded and spun around. The player tries to tack or tape the tail on the donkey, with each player's placement marked. The player making the most accurate placement wins.

Level of Activity: 2

Who: A,B,C,D

3 or more players

Location: indoor

PINCH ME

Preparation: Based on the number of players, prepare slips of paper with directions such as "Pinch me,"

"Tickle me," "Rub my tummy," "Scratch my back," "Pull my ear," etc. There should be an equal number in each group. Dark room.

How: All players must remain silent (no talking, but laughing is permitted). Each player receives a slip of paper, which is to be kept secret from the other players. Players are told the number in each group. The lights are turned off, and in the dark room the players proceed to try to find the members of their group by carrying out the directions of their slip. For example, a "Pinch me" would go around pinching people until another "Pinch me" is found. They then would work together to find the rest of the group. The first group completed wins.

Level of Activity: 3

Who: B,C,D

10 or more players

Location: indoor

PITCH AND CATCH

Preparation: One softball for each team. Mark two lines six to ten feet apart.

How: Players are divided into two or more teams. The teams line up behind the line designated as the catching line. One player on each team is given a softball and directed to stand on the second, or pitching, line, facing the player's own team. At the signal to begin, the pitcher tosses the ball to the facing team member, who catches it and runs to take the pitcher's place; the pitcher at the same time runs to the end of the team's line. This continues until all players have had a turn as pitcher and catcher. The team finishing first wins the game.

Level of Activity: 3

Who: B

8 or more players

Location: outdoor

PLATE SAILING

Preparation: Cardboard box; five paper plates.

How: Players take turns trying to sail the paper plates into the cardboard box from a distance of 10 to 15 feet. Each successful toss is scored as one point. The player with the most points wins the game. In the case of a tie there can be a play-off.

Level of Activity: 2

Who: B,C,D

2 or more players

Location: indoor, outdoor

POM POM PULLAWAY

Preparation: Establish two lines, 30 to 50 feet apart.

How: One player is "It" and stands in the middle of the playing area. All other players stand behind one line. "It" calls out "Pom Pom Pullaway! Come or I'll pull you away!" The players then try to reach the other line without being tagged by "It." Anyone tagged must join "It" and help tag other players until all are caught. The first person tagged is "It" for the next game.

Level of Activity: 3

Who: A,B

3 or more players

Location: outdoor

POOR PUSSY

Preparation: None.

How: One player is the Pussy. The other players form a circle, sitting around Pussy. Pussy moves on hands and knees to a player who must pet Pussy's head three times and say "Poor Pussy, poor Pussy, poor Pussy" without smiling. Pussy meows and tries to make the player smile. If Pussy is successful, the player must take Pussy's place.

Level of Activity: 2

Who: A,B,C

6 or more players

Location: indoor, outdoor

POSING

Preparation: None.

How: In pairs, players take turns posing for various situations determined by the other players. The two posers stand with their backs to the other players. The other players determine a situation and call it out, such as "a person meeting Dracula," "a person hearing a blackboard being scratched," "a teenager listening to rock music," etc. The posers turn around and act out the announced part.

Level of Activity: 2

Who: B,C,D

6 or more players

Location: indoor, outdoor

PROGRESSIVE STORY

Preparation: Pencil and large piece of paper for every fourth person.

How: Players sit in a circle; every fourth person is given a pencil and a sheet of paper and is told to write down the first line of a story and pass the pencil and paper to the person on the right, who adds another sentence, folds the paper so the first sentence is not visible and again passes the paper and pencil to the right. Each time the paper is passed, it is folded so that only the last line is visible. When the papers have gone around so that each has been written on by all the players, collect the papers and read the stories out loud.

Level of Activity: 1

Who: C,D

8 or more players

Location: indoor

PROPS

Preparation: Gather six or more unrelated objects as props for each team; paper and pencils.

How: Divide players into teams of three or more players each. Give each team its props, pencil and paper. Each team is to devise a dramatized story or skit involving the use of its props and to write it down within a set time. When the time is up, each team presents its story to the other group.

Level of Activity: 1

Who: D

8 or more players

Location: indoor

PUPPY RACE

Preparation: Establish start and finish lines 20 to 30 feet apart.

How: Players line up at the starting line on all fours. At the signal to start, the players head toward the finish line, barking as they go. The first player to reach the finish line wins the race.

Level of Activity: 3

Who: A,B

4 or more players

Location: outdoor

PUSSY WANTS A CORNER

Preparation: None.

How: Players go to corners of the room, except for one who is "It." "It" goes to a corner and says "Pussy wants a corner." The answer is always "Ask my neighbor." As Pussy moves on, players in two corners try to exchange corners. If Pussy can beat either of them to a corner, the person left out becomes the Pussy.

Level of Activity: 2

Who: B

5 or more players

Location: indoor

RED ROVER

Preparation: None.

How: The players are divided into two teams. The teams choose captains and then face each other, separated by about 20 feet. Team members form a chain by clasping hands. The captain of Team One calls out "Red Rover, Red Rover, send _____ over." The person called runs as fast as possible and tries to break through Team One's chain. If the runner breaks through, Team One loses one of its members to Team Two; if the runner does not break through the chain, the runner becomes a member of Team One. The captains alternate calling names until one team has been reduced to one member.

Level of Activity: 3

Who: B,C,D

8 or more players

Location: outdoor

RIBBON CUTTING

Preparation: Cut a supply of crepe paper ribbons, one for each team; a pair of rounded safety scissors for each team.

How: Players divide into teams of two players each. Each team member takes hold of an end of the streamer and stretches it out between them. At the signal to start, the team member with the scissors begins cutting the ribbon in half lengthwise, starting with the end in hand. Cutting should be continuous. If the ribbon is cut through to the edge, the team is disqualified. The first team with a continuously cut ribbon is the winner.

Level of Activity: 2

Who: B,C,D

4 or more players

Location: indoor

RING-AROUND-THE-ROSY

Preparation: None.

How: Players form a circle, hold hands and walk, singing:

"Ring-around-the-rosy,
Pocket full of posy,
Ashes, ashes, we all fall down."

On the word "down," all players fall to the floor.

Level of Activity: 2

Who: A

3 or more players

Location: indoor, outdoor

RING ON A STRING

Preparation: A string long enough to reach around the circle of players; a ring.

How: Players form a circle and pass the ring on the string from player to player. The person who is "It" is in the center of the circle and tries to determine who has the ring. "It" may ask any player to open one or both hands at any time. Players may attempt to fool "It" but must open hands whenever asked. When "It" identifies a player with the ring, they change places and the game proceeds.

Level of Activity: 2

Who: B,C,D

6 or more players

Location: indoor, outdoor

RING RELAY

Preparation: A supply of drinking straws, one for each player; a finger ring or Lifesaver candy for each team.

How: Players are divided into equal teams of four or more players each. The teams line up in columns, all facing the same direction. Players hold drinking straws in their mouths, and a finger ring or a Lifesaver is placed over the straw of the first player on each team. At a given signal, the first player turns around and, without the use of hands, transfers the ring or Lifesaver to the next player's straw. The ring is passed in this fashion to the end of each team line-up. The first team to finish wins the game. If the ring or Lifesaver drops, the players responsible must retrieve it by getting down on the floor and picking it up using only the straws in their mouths.

Level of Activity: 2

Who: B,C,D

8 or more even number
   of players

Location: indoor

S A R D I N E S

Preparation: Several rooms, preferably dark.

How: As with HIDE AND SEEK, SARDINES is played in several rooms, preferably in the dark. One player hides; the rest of the players seek out the hider. The first seeker to find the hider joins in hiding, both remaining as quiet as possible. The next successful seeker joins them, and so on. The game ends when all the "sardines" except one are wedged into the hiding area. The last one to discover the hiding area is the hider for the next game.

Level of Activity: 2

Who: B,C,D

4 or more players

Location: indoor

SCAVENGER HUNT

Preparation: Make lists of five or six things to find. These can be natural objects or items hidden away beforehand; for example, one paper clip, a large round stone, two blue flowers, a shoe, a white button.

How: Players are divided into teams of three. Each group holds hands and hunts together for the objects on its list. The winning team is the one that collects the objects on its list in the shortest time.

Level of Activity: 1

Who: B,C,D

At least 6 players

Location: outdoor

SCULPTOR

Preparation: None.

How: One player is selected as the Sculptor, who arranges all the other players in a variety of positions which must be held without moving. The Sculptor then goes up to each individual and attempts to make them smile, laugh or break the pose. The Sculptor may do anything short of touching the other players to make them smile, laugh or move. The first player to do so becomes the next Sculptor.

Level of Activity: 2

Who: B,C,D

5 or more players

Location: indoor, outdoor

SENSIBLE SENTENCE

Preparation: Paper and pencil for each player.

How: Each player takes a turn calling out a letter or two, depending on the number of players. Each player writes every letter as it is called out. The object is to compose a sensible sentence using the letters in the given order. For example:

W C M B Y G H
Will, call Mother before you get home.
or Willy can manage because you guide him.

Level of Activity: 1

Who: B,C,D

2 or more players

Location: indoor

SHADOW TAG

Preparation: None, but game requires sunshine.

How: One player is selected as "It." At the given signal, "It" chases the other players and tries to tag a player by stepping on the player's shadow and calling out the name of that particular player. The tagged player then becomes "It," and the game continues.

Level of Activity: 3

Who: B,C

4 or more players

Location: outdoor

SHARE THE TREAT

Preparation: The game can be played with enough bananas, marshmallows, or ice cream bars or other bars so that each player gets a portion; blindfolds for all players; a nonplaying starter/judge.

How: Players are divided into teams of two; players are seated opposite one another and blindfolded. When all players are ready, each is given one portion of the selected food. When the signal is given, the partners try to feed one another. The first pair to successfully finish the feeding task wins the contest.

Level of Activity: 1

Who: B,C,D

4 or more players

Location: indoor, outdoor

SHOE MATCH

Preparation: Box large enough to hold one shoe from each player.

How: Each player removes one shoe and places it in the box. Everyone picks out someone else's shoe and, while holding the shoe, joins hands. The players then try to locate the owner of the shoe they are holding and return the shoe without letting go of each other's hands.

Level of Activity: 2

Who: A

5 or more players

Location: indoor

SHOE PUT

Preparation: Starting line.

How: Players line up at the starting line. Each player loosens one shoe so that it hangs off the end of the foot. At an agreed signal, each player kicks the loose shoe as far as possible. The farthest kick wins.

Level of Activity: 3

Who: B,C,D

3 or more players

Location: outdoor

SHOE SCRAMBLE

Preparation: None.

How: Each player removes shoes and places in a pile. The players move to a starting line 10 to 15 feet away, and at the signal the players try to retrieve and put on their own shoes (not necessary to tie or buckle). The first player back to the starting line wins.

Level of Activity: 3

Who: A

3 or more players

Location: indoor, outdoor

SIMON SAYS

Preparation: None.

How: One player is "Simon." The rest of the players stand throughout the playing area to allow ample room for action. "Simon" gives commands such as "Simon says put your hand on your head," "Simon says do a jumping jack," etc. Players obey the commands, except when "Simon" neglects to say "Simon says. . . ." Any player who does a command not prefaced by "Simon says" or who does not immediately obey a complete command must drop out of the game. The last player remaining becomes the next "Simon." "Simon" can make the game more difficult by performing all the actions.

Level of Activity: 3

Who: A,B,C

4 or more players

Location: indoor, outdoor

SING ALONG

Preparation: Enough slips of paper so there is one for each player. Write the titles of popular songs on the slips, making several slips for each title.

How: This is a mixer to start a party. Each player selects a slip of paper. The players proceed to try to identify others in their respective song group. When the groups have gathered together, each group takes turns singing its particular song.

Level of Activity: 2

Who: B,C,D

10 or more players

Location: indoor, outdoor

SOUNDS LIKE

Preparation: Prepare a variety of opaque containers by placing in each one something that will rattle when the container is shaken (e.g., rice, coins, small bells). Number each container. Paper and pencil for each player.

How: Players try to decide what each container holds by shaking it. Guesses are written down by each player. The player with the greatest number of correct guesses wins the game.

Level of Activity: 1

Who: B,C,D

3 or more players

Location: indoor

SPELLOUT

Preparation: None.

How: One player is selected as "It." "It" stands in a circle of the other players. "It" spells a short word (three to five letters) and points to a player in the circle. The player pointed to must quickly name an object starting with each of the letters used to spell the word. For example, "C A T": "Cartoon, Apple, Turtle." If the player pointed to cannot think of a word or takes too long, the player trades places with "It."

Level of Activity: 1

Who: B,C

6 or more players

Location: indoor

SPIDER WEB

Preparation: Tie a small prize to the end of a ball of string (approximately 15 feet long), preparing one ball for each player. Unwind the string, passing over and around objects in the play area.

How: Each player takes the end of the string and proceeds to rewind it until the prize at the end is found.

Level of Activity: 2

Who: A,B

2 or more players

Location: indoor, outdoor

SQUAT TAG

Preparation: None.

How: One player is designated "It"; the other players scatter over the game area. The only way to avoid being tagged is to squat down and call out "Squat!" "It" tries to tag one of the players in order to exchange places.

Level of Activity: 3

Who: A,B,C

4 or more players

Location: outdoor

SQUIRREL IN A TREE

Preparation: None.

How: Except for "It," players count off into groups of three. The Ones and Twos form trees. The Threes are squirrels inside the trees. "It" is a squirrel looking for a tree. At the signal from a leader, all squirrels must change trees, and "It" tries to take the place of one of them. After several rounds, reassign roles so that all players have an equal opportunity to be squirrels.

Level of Activity: 3

Who: B,C,D

8 or more players

Location: spacious indoor
area, outdoor

STATUES

Preparation: None.

How: One player is selected as "It" and stands at one end of the playing area, facing away from the other players. The other players go to the other end of the area and at a given signal attempt to advance on the player who is "It." "It" may turn around at any time, and if players are detected in motion, they must return to the starting line. The player getting close enough to tag "It" without being caught is the next "It."

Level of Activity: 2

Who: B,C,D

4 or more players

Location: indoor, outdoor

STRING RELAY

Preparation: Two balls of string.

How: This is a two-part game. Players are divided into two equal teams. Each team lines up, one player behind another player. The first player on each team is given a ball of string and, at a signal, the ball of string is passed down one side of each team line and up the other. This continues until the balls of string are used up. The first team to unwind the string wins the first part of the game. The second part of the game reverses the process, and the first team to rewind the string is declared the winner.

Level of Activity: 2

Who: B,C

6 or more players

Location: indoor, outdoor

SUITCASE RELAY

Preparation: Two suitcases; at least three articles of similar clothing for each.

How: Players are divided into two teams, and each team forms a line facing the other team. The first person in each line is given a suitcase. At the signal to start, the person opens the suitcase and puts on the clothes, fastens them, takes them off and returns them to the suitcase, which is then passed down to the next person in line, who does the same thing. The team finishing first is the winner.

Level of Activity: 3

Who: B,C,D

8 or more players

Location: indoor, outdoor

T A G

Preparation: None.

How: One player is "It" and tries to tag any other player. Any player tagged becomes the new "It." Players may establish a "safety" area if desired.

Level of Activity: 3

Who: A,B

3 or more players

Location: outdoor

" 1 0 "

Preparation: Several small gift objects, such as coins, candy, keychains, or pens.

How: This is a mixer to start a party where the guests are not well acquainted. The small gift objects are distributed to several players, and it is announced that this has been done and that the individual objects will be given to the tenth player who shakes hands with the holder of each of the objects.

89

Level of Activity: 2

Who: B,C,D

10 or more players

Location: indoor, outdoor

THINGS

Preparation: Paper and pencils for all players; timer.

How: Players select four letters of the alphabet and write the letters on their paper. At the signal, players write on their sheets the names of objects visible in the room that begin with those letters. At the end of 15 minutes, the player with the longest accurate list is the winner.

Level of Activity: 1

Who: C,D

4 or more players

Location: indoor

TICK TOCK

Preparation: A small clock with a loud tick, hidden in the play area.

How: Players try to locate the clock. The first one who does is the winner.

Level of Activity: 2

Who: B

4 or more players

Location: indoor

TOY SHOP

Preparation: None.

How: One player is the store clerk, another the customer, and the rest are "toys." The customer leaves the area while the store clerk and other players decide what "toys" will be in the store. The customer returns and asks to see toys, such as a doll, roller skates, etc. The customer gets two chances to identify a "toy" in the shop. If a correct guess is made, the identified toy imitates that toy's action before exchanging places with the customer, and a new game is begun.

Level of Activity: 2

Who: A,B

5 or more players

Location: indoor, outdoor

TREASURE HUNT

Preparation: Determine what the "treasure" will be and where to place it. Prepare 10 to 15 clues leading to the treasure.

How: Hunters work in pairs. All get the first clue and set out at the same time to locate the rest of the clues which lead ultimately to the treasure. Set a definite time limit to the hunt.

Level of Activity: 2

Who: B,C,D

6 or more players

Location: indoor, outdoor

TWENTY QUESTIONS

Preparation: None.

How: One player chooses the name of any object. All other players then ask questions trying to guess the object. They are allowed 20 questions that can be answered "Yes," "No," or "I don't know." The player answering keeps track of the number of questions asked. The first person guessing the object wins and may select the next object.

Level of Activity: 1

Who: B,C,D

5 or more players

Location: indoor

UMBRELLA BALL

Preparation: Tennis ball, umbrella.

How: Place an open umbrella upside-down approximately 10 to 15 feet away from the starting line. Players take turns standing at the starting line and trying to bounce the tennis ball into the umbrella so that it stays there. Each successful bounce is worth one point; the first player to reach 10 points is declared the winner.

Level of Activity: 2

Who: B,C,D

2 or more players

Location: indoor

UP, JENKINS!

Preparation: Coin, table and chairs.

How: Players divide into two teams. Each team then sits on opposite sides of the table. Team One takes the coin and passes it from player to player under the table. When Team Two calls "Up, Jenkins!", all players on Team One raise closed fists over the table. Team Two then calls "Down, Jenkins!", and Team One players place their hands, palm down, on the table. Team Two players consult each other to try to decide which hand the coin is under. Guesses continue until the coin is found. Team Two players then hide the coin. The game may proceed as long as desired, with the team making the least number of guesses the winner.

Level of Activity: 2

Who: B,C,D

6 or more players

Location: indoor, outdoor

WALKING GAME

Preparation: None.

How: Keeping pace with each other, the players choose a point some distance away, and each estimates how many steps it will take to reach the point. Players then set out keeping pace with one another, each counting off the steps taken. After several trials, accuracy will greatly increase, and players may want to choose points farther away for greater difficulty. The player with the closest estimate wins the game.

Level of Activity: 2

Who: B,C,D

2 or more players

Location: outdoor

WASTEBASKET BALL

Preparation: Tennis ball; wastebasket; straight-back chair.

How: The wastebasket is placed eight feet from the starting line; the chair is placed about three feet in front of the wastebasket. Players in turn stand at the starting line and try to bounce the tennis ball between themselves and the chair in such a way that it will go over the chair and land in the wastebasket. If the ball stays in the basket, the player earns ten points. If the ball bounces into the basket and out again, the player earns five points. Each player is allowed four chances; the one with the highest score wins the game.

Level of Activity: 1

Who: B,C,D

3 or more players

Location: indoor

WHAT AM I DOING?

Preparation: None.

How: Three players are sent from the room. While they are gone, the other players decide on an action, e.g., washing a car, hanging wallpaper, playing a sport. One player is selected to demonstrate the action for the first player, who has been asked to return to the room. Player number One then demonstrates the action for player Two, and player number Two for player Three. Player Three then guesses what the action is. If wrong, player Two guesses, and if Two is wrong, player One guesses. If all three players guess wrong, the group tells them what action was demonstrated.

Level of Activity: 2

Who: C,D

8 or more players

Location: indoor

WHAT ANIMAL AM I?

Preparation: Wrap as many different animal crackers as there are players; place in bowl.

How: Players form a circle. Each player selects one wrapped animal cracker and unwraps the animal cracker but does not let the other players see it. Players take turns standing inside the circle, acting like the animal on the player's cracker. The other players then try to guess which animal is being imitated.

Level of Activity: 2

Who: A,B

4 or more players

Location: indoor

WHAT WORD?

Preparation: None.

How: One player is selected as "It." "It" thinks of a word and then announces to the other players, "I am thinking of a word that rhymes with _____." The other players take turns to try to guess the word. The first player guessing correctly replaces "It," and the game goes on.

Level of Activity: 1

Who: B,C,D

3 or more players

Location: indoor

WHERE AM I?

Preparation: None.

How: One player is selected as "It." "It" selects an imaginary place to "hide" and asks the question "Where am I?" Players ask questions to narrow the scope of the hunt. "It" is required to answer "Yes" or "No." "It" wins if the other players take more than five minutes to guess the "hiding place." "Hiding places" may be limited geographically to narrow the search for the players doing the questioning.

Level of Activity: 1

Who: B,C,D

4 or more players

Location: indoor

WHO AM I?

Preparation: Write the name of a famous person on a slip of paper, one for each player. One pin for each player.

How: Pin a name to the back of each player. The players each try to guess the famous name on their backs by asking such questions as "Am I alive?", "Am I a movie star?", "Am I a politician?"

Level of Activity: 2

Who: C,D

4 or more players

Location: indoor, outdoor

WORD MATCH I

Preparation: Make up 4" x 6" cards using short words that pair easily (e.g., basket, ball, barn, yard, every, one, some, thing, foot, print).

How: Each player selects a card and tries to find someone else with a matching word to make a double
word. There may be more than one combination of
words possible. This is a good icebreaker game.

Level of Activity: 2

Who: B,C,D

6 or more players

Location: indoor, outdoor

WORD MATCH II

Preparation: A list of familiar quotations or pairs is
compiled. Each quotation or pair is to be written
so that by joining the two cards, the thought is
completed.

How: This is a mixer to start a party. Each player
selects a slip of paper and tries to match up with
the other half, which is held by another player.

Level of Activity: 2

Who: C,D

10 or more players

Location: indoor, outdoor

YES AND NO

Preparation: 10 small items--marbles, pennies, beans or
something similar--for each player.

How: No one is to use the words "Yes" or "No." Each
player receives 10 items and takes a turn as
questioner. Each time a player says "Yes" or "No"
to a question, one item is forfeited. After a
designated amount of time, the player with the
most items is declared the winner.

Level of Activity: 1

Who: B,C,D

3 or more players

Location: indoor, outdoor

YOU'VE GOT A . . .

Preparation: None.

How: A player begins by turning to the player on the left and saying "You've got a (foot, dog, coat or such item)," to which the second player replies, "What sort of (item)?" The first player responds, for example, with "A fantastic foot." The game goes on, with each player answering the question with an adjective beginning with the same letter the first player used.

Level of Activity: 1

Who: B,C,D

3 or more players

Location: indoor

Index to Games by Age Level

PRESCHOOL - AGE 7

Title	Activity Level	Age Level	Players	Indoor	Out
Airplane Race	2	ABC	6 +	I	O
Ball Roll	2	A	3 +	I	O
Bellringer	2	AB	4 +		O
Birds Fly	2	AB	3 +	I	O
Chain Tag	3	ABC	4 +		O
Charley Over the Water	3	AB	6 +	I	O
Circle Race	3	ABC	3 +		O
Coin Drop	1	AB	2 +	I	
Colors	1	A	2 +	I	
Cooperative Art	2	ABC	4 +	I	
Drop the Handkerchief	3	ABC	6 +	I	O
Duck, Duck, Gray Duck	3	AB	4 +	I	O
Fabric Match	1	AB	2 +	I	O
Farmer in the Dell	2	AB	8 +	I	O
Fishing for Paper Clips	2	ABC	2 +	I	
Follow the Leader	3	ABCD	4 +	I	O
Food for Thought	1	AB	2 +	I	O
Group Hide and Seek	2	AB	4 +	I	O
Group Musical Chairs	3	AB	4 +	I	O
Hide and Seek	2	AB	4 +	I	O
Hot and Cold	2	AB	2 +	I	
Hot Money	2	ABC	8 +	I	O
Indoor Football	2	ABCD	4 +	I	
Laughing	2	ABCD	5 +	I	O
Letter Trace	1	AB	2 +	I	O
London Bridge	2	A	4 +	I	O
Pass It On	2	ABC	6 +	I	O
Pass the Prize	2	AB	5 +	I	O
Pin the Tail on the Donkey	2	ABCD	3 +	I	
Pom Pom Pullaway	3	AB	3 +		O
Poor Pussy	2	ABC	6 +	I	O
Puppy Race	3	AB	4 +		O
Ring-Around-the-Rosy	2	A	3 +	I	O
Shoe Match	2	A	5 +	I	
Shoe Scramble	3	A	3 +	I	O
Simon Says	3	ABC	4 +	I	O
Spider Web	2	AB	2 +	I	O
Squat Tag	3	ABC	4 +		O
Tag	3	AB	3 +		O

				Indoor	Out
Toy Shop	2	AB	5 +	I	O
What Animal Am I?	2	AB	4 +	I	

AGES 8 – 12

Title	Activity Level	Age Level	Players	WHERE? Indoor	Out
Air, Land, Water	1	B C	5 +	I	O
Airplane Race	2	AB C	6 +	I	O
Alphabet Adjectives	1	B C D	4 +	I	
Amoeba	3	B C D	6 +		O
Are You Out There?	2	B C D	8 +	I	O
Arise	2	B C	2 +	I	O
Arise for Two	2	B C	6 +	I	O
Artists	2	B C D	4 +	I	
At Sea	3	B C D	8 +	I	O
Backward Bowling	2	B C	2 +		O
Balancing the Books	2	B C	3 +	I	
Balloon Ball	3	B C	8 +	I	
Balloon Break	3	B C D	4 +	I	O
Balloon Relay	3	B C D	6 +	I	O
Balloon Volleyball	3	B C D	4 +		O
Barnyard Buddy	2	B C	8 +	I	O
Bean Transfer	2	B C	6 +	I	
Bell Bluff	2	B C D	6 +	I	
Bellringer	2	AB	4 +		O
Bird, Beast or Fish	1	B C D	6 +	I	O
Birds Fly	2	AB	3 +	I	O
Blind Man's Bluff	2	B C D	6 +	I	O
Bottle Answer	1	B C D	5 +	I	
Bounce	2	B C	2 +	I	O
Button Sort	2	B C	3 +	I	
Call Ball	3	B C	4 +		O
Call Out Ball	3	B C	6 +		O
Captain, May I?	2	B	5 +	I	O
Capture	2	B C	8 +	I	O
Capture the Flag	3	B	6 +	I	O
Card Toss	1	B C	4 +	I	
Cat and Dog	2	B C D	2 +	I	
Cat and Mice	3	B	8 +		O
Cat and Mouse	3	B C	10 +	I	O
Catch Ball	3	B C	10 +		O
Caterpillar Race	3	B C	8 +		O
Cause and Effect	1	B C D	3 +	I	
Celebrities	2	B C	4 +	I	
Chain Tag	3	AB C	4 +		O
Chain Words	2	B C D	5 +	I	O
Change Partners	2	B C	7 +	I	O
Charley Over the Water	3	AB	6 +	I	O
Circle Race	3	AB C	3 +		O
Circle Tug of War	3	B C D	8 +		O

Game					
In This House	1	B C	3 +	I	
Indoor Football	2	AB CD	4 +	I	
Kangaroo Race	3	B C	3 +	I	O
Keep Away	3	B C	3 +		O
Kerchief Grab	3	B C	6 +	I	
Kerchief Relay	3	B	10 +	I	O
Laughing	2	AB CD	5 +	I	O
Letter Trace	1	AB	2 +	I	O
Lifesaver Relay	2	B CD	8 +	I	
Look and Remember	1	B C	3 +	I	O
Making Squares	1	B CD	2 +	I	
Marble Golf	2	B C	3 +		O
Mrs. O'Leary's Cow	1	B CD	3 +	I	
Musical Chairs	3	B CD	5 +	I	
Nursery Rhyme	1	B	2 +	I	
Packing for a Trip	1	B CD	6 +	I	O
Pair Tag	3	B C	6 +		O
Paper, Scissors, Stone	2	B C	2 +	I	O
Pass It On	2	AB C	6 +	I	O
Pass the Prize	2	AB	5 +	I	O
Peanut Drop	1	B CD	3 +	I	
Peanut Relay	2	B CD	6 +	I	O
People Puzzle	2	B CD	6 +	I	O
Pickle in the Middle	3	B	3	I	O
Pin the Tail on the Donkey	2	AB CD	3 +	I	
Pinch Me	3	B CD	10 +	I	
Pitch and Catch	3	B	8 +		O
Plate Sailing	2	B CD	2 +	I	O
Pom Pom Pullaway	3	AB	3 +		O
Poor Pussy	2	AB C	6 +	I	O
Posing	2	B CD	6 +	I	O
Puppy Race	3	AB	4 +		O
Pussy Wants a Corner	2	B	5 +	I	
Red Rover	3	B CD	8 +		O
Ribbon Cutting	2	B CD	4 +	I	
Ring on a String	2	B CD	6 +	I	O
Ring Relay	2	B CD	8 +	I	
Sardines	2	B CD	4 +	I	
Scavenger Hunt	1	B CD	6 +		O
Sculptor	2	B CD	5 +	I	O
Sensible Sentence	1	B CD	2 +	I	
Shadow Tag	3	B C	4 +		O
Share the Treat	1	B CD	4 +	I	O
Shoe Put	3	B CD	3 +		O
Simon Says	3	AB C	4 +	I	O
Sing Along	2	B CD	10 +	I	O
Sounds Like	1	B CD	3 +	I	
Spellout	1	B C	6 +	I	
Spider Web	2	AB	2 +	I	O
Squat Tag	3	AB C	4 +		O
Squirrel in a Tree	3	B CD	8 +	I	O
Statues	2	B CD	4 +	I	O
String Relay	2	B C	6 +	I	O

102

TEEN-AGE

Cat and Mouse	3	B C	10 +	I	O
Catch Ball	3	B C	10 +		O
Categories	1	C D	3 +	I	
Caterpillar Race	3	B C	8 +		O
Cause and Effect	1	B C D	3 +	I	
Celebrities	2	B C	4 +	I	
Chain Tag	3	A B C	4 +		O
Chain Words	2	B C D	5 +	I	O
Change Partners	2	B C	7 +	I	O
Chin Game	2	C D	8 +	I	O
Circle Race	3	A B C	3 +		O
Circle Tug of War	3	B C D	8 +		O
Coat and Hat Relay	3	B C	8 +		O
Coin Collector	1	B C D	4 +	I	
Compliments	1	B C D	4 +	I	
Contrary Actions	2	B C D	4 +	I	O
Cooperative Art	2	A B C	4 +	I	
Cooperative Tale	1	B C D	4 +	I	O
Dot Art	2	B C D	3 +	I	
Dramatic Poetry	1	B C D	4 +	I	
Draw the Tail on the Donkey	2	B C D	3 +	I	
Drop the Handkerchief	3	A B C	6 +	I	O
Duet	2	B C D	6 +	I	O
Egg Race	2	B C D	4 +	I	O
Famous Names	1	B C D	4 +	I	
Feather Float	3	B C D	8 +	I	O
Find It	2	B C D	6 +	I	
Fire Chief	3	B C	13 +		O
Fish	3	B C D	4 +	I	O
Fishing for Paper Clips	2	A B C	2 +	I	
Follow the Leader	3	A B C D	4 +	I	O
Forbidden Word	1	B C D	4 +	I	
Glove Relay	2	B C D	6 +	I	
Good Morning!	2	B C	6 +	I	O
Grandmother's Trunk	1	B C D	3 +	I	O
Groups	2	B C	10 +	I	O
Guess Ball	2	B C	4 +	I	O
Guess the Leader	2	B C D	6 +	I	
Guessing Contest	1	B C D	4 +	I	O
Ha, Ha, Ha	1	B C D	5 +	I	O
Hangman	1	B C D	2 +	I	
Hat Exchange	2	B C D	6 +		
Have You Seen My Friend?	3	B C	6 +	I	O
Holiday	1	B C	6 +	I	
Hot Money	2	A B C	8 +	I	O
Hot Potato	2	B C D	5 +	I	O
How Do You Like Your Neighbors?	2	B C D	5 +	I	O
Howdy, Neighbor	2	B C D	10 +		O
Hunt the Thimble	2	B C D	4 +	I	
Hunters and Hunted	3	B C	8 +	I	O

Title	Activity Level	Age Level	Players	Indoor	Out
Twenty Questions	1	B C D	5 +	I	
Umbrella Ball	2	B C D	2 +	I	
Up, Jenkins!	2	B C D	6 +	I	O
Walking Game	2	B C D	2 +		O
Wastebasket Ball	1	B C D	3 +	I	
What Am I Doing?	2	C D	8 +	I	
What Word?	1	B C D	3 +	I	
Where Am I?	1	B C D	4 +	I	
Who Am I?	2	C D	4 +	I	O
Word Match I	2	B C D	6 +	I	O
Word Match II	2	C D	10 +	I	O
Yes and No	1	B C D	3 +	I	O
You've Got a...	1	B C D	3 +	I	O

ADULT

Title	Activity Level	Age Level	Players	WHERE? Indoor	Out
Adverbs	1	D	4 +	I	
Advertisements	1	C D	5 +	I	O
Affinities	1	C D	4 +	I	
Alphabet Adjectives	1	B C D	4 +	I	
Amoeba	3	B C D	6 +		O
Are You Out There?	2	B C D	8 +	I	O
Artists	2	B C D	4 +	I	
At Sea	3	B C D	8 +	I	O
Balloon Break	3	B C D	4 +	I	O
Balloon Relay	3	B C D	6 +	I	O
Balloon Volleyball	3	B C D	4 +		O
Bell Bluff	2	B C D	6 +	I	
Bird, Beast or Fish	1	B C D	6 +	I	O
Blind Man's Bluff	2	B C D	6 +	I	O
Bottle Answer	1	B C D	5 +	I	
Cat and Dog	2	B C D	2 +	I	
Categories	1	C D	3 +	I	
Cause and Effect	1	B C D	3 +	I	
Chain Words	2	B C D	5 +	I	O
Chin Game	2	C D	8 +	I	O
Circle Tug of War	3	B C D	8 +		O
Coin Collector	1	B C D	4 +	I	
Compliments	1	B C D	4 +	I	
Contrary Actions	2	B C D	4 +	I	O
Cooperative Tale	1	B C D	4 +	I	O
Dot Art	2	B C D	3 +	I	
Double Words	1	D	2 +	I	
Dramatic Poetry	1	B C D	4 +	I	
Draw the Tail on the Donkey	2	B C D	3 +	I	
Duet	2	B C D	6 +	I	O
Egg Race	2	B C D	4 +	I	O
Famous Names	1	B C D	4 +	I	

Suitcase Relay	3	B C D	8 +	I	O
"10"	2	B C D	10 +	I	O
Things	1	C D	4 +	I	
Treasure Hunt	2	B C D	6 +	I	O
Twenty Questions	1	B C D	5 +	I	
Umbrella Ball	2	B C D	2 +	I	
Up, Jenkins!	2	B C D	6 +	I	O
Walking Game	2	B C D	2 +		O
Wastebasket Ball	1	B C D	3 +	I	
What Am I Doing?	2	C D	8 +	I	
What Word?	1	B C D	3 +	I	
Where Am I?	1	B C D	4 +	I	
Who Am I?	2	C D	4 +	I	O
Word Match I	2	B C D	6 +	I	O
Word Match II	2	C D	10 +	I	O
Yes and No	1	B C D	3 +	I	O
You've Got a...	1	B C D	3 +	I	

Index to Games by Level of Activity

LITTLE ACTIVITY

Title	Activity Level	Age Level	Players	Indoor	Out
Adverbs	1	D	4 +	I	
Advertisements	1	CD	5 +	I	O
Affinities	1	CD	4 +	I	
Air, Land, Water	1	BC	5 +	I	O
Alphabet Adjectives	1	BCD	4 +	I	
Bird, Beast or Fish	1	BCD	6 +	I	O
Bottle Answer	1	BCD	5 +	I	
Card Toss	1	BC	4 +	I	
Categories	1	CD	3 +	I	
Cause and Effect	1	BCD	3 +	I	
Coin Collector	1	BCD	4 +	I	
Coin Drop	1	AB	2 +	I	
Colors	1	A	2 +	I	
Compliments	1	BCD	4 +	I	
Cooperative Tale	1	BCD	4 +	I	O
Double Words	1	D	2 +	I	
Dramatic Poetry	1	BCD	4 +	I	
Fabric Match	1	AB	2 +	I	O
Famous Names	1	BCD	4 +	I	
Food for Thought	1	AB	2 +	I	O
Forbidden Word	1	BCD	4 +	I	
Grandmother's Trunk	1	BCD	3 +	I	O
Guessing Contest	1	BCD	4 +	I	O
Ha, Ha, Ha	1	BCD	5 +	I	O
Hangman	1	BCD	2 +	I	
Holiday	1	BC	6 +	I	
I Don't Like...	1	CD	4 +	I	
I Love My Love	1	CD	4 +	I	
In This House	1	BC	3 +	I	
Indoor Scavenger Hunt	1	D	6 +	I	
Letter Trace	1	AB	2 +	I	O
Look and Remember	1	BC	3 +	I	O
Making Squares	1	BCD	2 +	I	
Mrs. O'Leary's Cow	1	BCD	3 +	I	
Nursery Rhyme	1	B	2 +	I	
Packing for a Trip	1	BCD	6 +	I	O
Peanut Drop	1	BCD	3 +	I	
Progressive Story	1	CD	8 +	I	
Props	1	D	8 +	I	

Scavenger Hunt	1	B CD	6 +	O
Sensible Sentence	1	B CD	2 +	I
Share the Treat	1	B CD	4 +	I O
Sounds Like	1	B CD	3 +	I
Spellout	1	B C	6 +	I
Things	1	CD	4 +	I
Twenty Questions	1	B CD	5 +	I
Wastebasket Ball	1	B CD	3 +	I
What Word?	1	B CD	3 +	I
Where Am I?	1	B CD	4 +	I
Yes and No	1	B CD	3 +	I O
You've Got a...	1	B CD	3 +	I

MODERATE ACTIVITY

Title	Activity Level	Age Level	Players	Indoor	Out
Airplane Race	2	AB C	6 +	I	O
Are You Out There?	2	B CD	8 +	I	O
Arise	2	B C	2 +	I	O
Arise for Two	2	B C	6 +	I	O
Artists	2	B CD	4 +	I	
Backward Bowling	2	B C	2 +		O
Balancing the Books	2	B C	3 +	I	
Ball Roll	2	A	3 +	I	O
Barnyard Buddy	2	B C	8 +	I	O
Bean Transfer	2	B C	6 +	I	
Bell Bluff	2	B CD	6 +	I	
Bellringer	2	AB	4 +		O
Birds Fly	2	AB	3 +	I	O
Blind Man's Bluff	2	B CD	6 +	I	O
Bounce	2	B C	2 +	I	O
Button Sort	2	B C	3 +	I	
Captain, May I?	2	B	5 +	I	O
Capture	2	B C	8 +	I	O
Cat and Dog	2	B CD	2 +	I	
Celebrities	2	B C	4 +	I	
Chain Words	2	B CD	5 +	I	O
Change Partners	2	B C	7 +	I	O
Chin Game	2	CD	8 +	I	O
Contrary Actions	2	B CD	4 +	I	O
Cooperative Art	2	AB C	4 +	I	
Dark Draw	2	B	3 +	I	
Dot Art	2	B CD	3 +	I	
Draw the Tail on the Donkey	2	B CD	3 +	I	
Duet	2	B CD	6 +	I	O
Egg Race	2	B CD	4 +	I	O
Farmer in the Dell	2	AB	8 +	I	O
Find It	2	B CD	6 +	I	
Fishing for Paper Clips	2	AB C	2 +	I	

Who Am I?	2	CD	4 +	I	O
Word Match I	2	BCD	6 +	I	O
Word Match II	2	CD	10 +	I	O

MUCH ACTIVITY

Title	Activity Level	Age Level	Players	WHERE? Indoor	Out
Amoeba	3	BCD	6 +		O
At Sea	3	BCD	8 +	I	O
Balloon Ball	3	BC	8 +	I	
Balloon Break	3	BCD	4 +	I	O
Balloon Relay	3	BCD	6 +	I	O
Balloon Volleyball	3	BCD	4 +		O
Call Ball	3	BC	4 +		O
Call Out Ball	3	BC	6 +		O
Capture the Flag	3	B	6 +	I	O
Cat and Mice	3	B	8 +		O
Cat and Mouse	3	BC	10 +	I	O
Catch Ball	3	BC	10 +		O
Caterpillar Race	3	BC	8 +		O
Chain Tag	3	ABC	4 +		O
Charley Over the Water	3	AB	6 +	I	O
Circle Race	3	ABC	3 +		O
Circle Tug of War	3	BCD	8 +		O
Coat and Hat Relay	3	BC	8 +		O
Drop the Handkerchief	3	ABC	6 +	I	O
Duck, Duck, Gray Duck	3	AB	4 +	I	O
Duck Walk	3	B	2 +	I	O
Feather Float	3	BCD	8 +	I	O
Fire Chief	3	BC	13 +		O
Fish	3	BCD	4 +	I	O
Follow the Leader	3	ABCD	4 +	I	O
Go Find the Swatter	3	B	5 +	I	O
Group Musical Chairs	3	AB	4 +	I	O
Have You Seen My Friend?	3	BC	6 +	I	O
Hunters and Hunted	3	BC	8 +	I	O
Kangaroo Race	3	BC	3 +	I	O
Keep Away	3	BC	3 +		O
Kerchief Grab	3	BC	6 +	I	
Kerchief Relay	3	B	10 +	I	O
Musical Chairs	3	BCD	5 +	I	
Pair Tag	3	BC	6 +		O
Pickle in the Middle	3	B	3	I	O
Pinch Me	3	BCD	10 +	I	
Pitch and Catch	3	B	8 +		O
Pom Pom Pullaway	3	AB	3 +		O
Puppy Race	3	AB	4 +		O
Red Rover	3	BCD	8 +		O
Shadow Tag	3	BC	4 +		O

Index by Level of Activity

Index to Games by Type

ATHLETIC GAMES

Title	Activity Level	Age Level	Players	WHERE? Indoor	Out
Amoeba	3	B CD	6 +		O
Arise	2	B C	2 +	I	O
Arise for Two	2	B C	6 +	I	O
At Sea	3	B CD	8 +	I	O
Backward Bowling	2	B C	2 +		O
Balloon Ball	3	B C	8 +	I	
Balloon Break	3	B CD	4 +	I	O
Balloon Relay	3	B CD	6 +	I	O
Balloon Volleyball	3	B CD	4 +		O
Bellringer	2	AB	4 +		O
Call Ball	3	B C	4 +		O
Call Out Ball	3	B C	6 +		O
Capture	2	B C	8 +	I	O
Capture the Flag	3	B	6 +	I	O
Cat and Dog	2	B CD	2 +	I	
Cat and Mice	3	B	8 +		O
Cat and Mouse	3	B C	10 +	I	O
Catch Ball	3	B C	10 +		O
Caterpillar Race	3	B C	8 +		O
Chain Tag	3	AB C	4 +		O
Charley Over the Water	3	AB	6 +	I	O
Chin Game	2	CD	8 +	I	O
Circle Race	3	AB C	3 +		O
Circle Tug of War	3	B CD	8 +		O
Coat and Hat Relay	3	B C	8 +		O
Contrary Actions	2	B CD	4 +	I	O
Drop the Handkerchief	3	AB C	6 +	I	O
Duck, Duck, Gray Duck	3	AB	4 +	I	O
Duck Walk	3	B	2 +	I	O
Egg Race	2	B CD	4 +	I	O
Fire Chief	3	B C	13 +		O
Fish	3	B CD	4 +	I	O
Follow the Leader	3	AB CD	4 +	I	O
Go Find the Swatter	3	B	5 +	I	O
Group Musical Chairs	3	AB	4 +	I	O
Groups	2	B C	10 +	I	O
Have You Seen My Friend?	3	B C	6 +	I	O
Hide and Seek	2	AB	4 +	I	O

115

How Do You Like Your Neighbors?	2	B CD	5 +	I	O
Howdy, Neighbor	2	B CD	10 +		O
Hunters and Hunted	3	B C	8 +	I	O
Kangaroo Race	3	B C	3 +	I	O
Keep Away	3	B C	3 +		O
Kerchief Grab	3	B C	6 +	I	
Kerchief Relay	3	B	10 +	I	O
Musical Chairs	3	B CD	5 +	I	
Pair Tag	3	B C	6 +		O
Pickle in the Middle	3	B	3	I	O
Pitch and Catch	3	B	8 +		O
Pom Pom Pullaway	3	AB	3 +		O
Puppy Race	3	AB	4 +		O
Pussy Wants a Corner	2	B	5 +	I	
Red Rover	3	B CD	8 +		O
Ring-Around-the-Rosy	2	A	3 +	I	O
Shadow Tag	3	B C	4 +		O
Shoe Scramble	3	A	3 +	I	O
Squat Tag	3	AB C	4 +		O
Squirrel in a Tree	3	B CD	8 +	I	O
Statues	2	B CD	4 +	I	O
Suitcase Relay	3	B CD	8 +	I	O
Tag	3	AB	3 +		O

BALL GAMES

Title	Activity Level	Age Level	Players	WHERE? Indoor	Out
Backward Bowling	2	B C	2 +		O
Ball Roll	2	A	3 +	I	O
Bellringer	2	AB	4 +		O
Call Ball	3	B C	4 +		O
Call Out Ball	3	B C	6 +		O
Catch Ball	3	B C	10 +		O
Chain Words	2	B CD	5 +	I	O
Chin Game	2	CD	8 +	I	O
Egg Race	2	B CD	4 +	I	O
Guess Ball	2	B C	4 +	I	O
Hot Potato	2	B CD	5 +	I	O
Indoor Football	2	AB CD	4 +	I	
Keep Away	3	B C	3 +		O
Pickle in the Middle	3	B	3	I	O
Pitch and Catch	3	B	8 +		O
Umbrella Ball	2	B CD	2 +	I	
Wastebasket Ball	1	B CD	3 +	I	

116

Index to Games by Type

BALLOON GAMES

Title	Activity Level	Age Level	Players	WHERE? Indoor	Out
Balloon Ball	3	B C	8 +	I	
Balloon Break	3	B CD	4 +	I	O
Balloon Relay	3	B CD	6 +	I	O
Balloon Volleyball	3	B CD	4 +		O
Catch Ball	3	B C	10 +		O
Indoor Football	2	AB CD	4 +	I	
Kangaroo Race	3	B C	3 +	I	O
Keep Away	3	B C	3 +		O

BLINDFOLD GAMES

Title	Activity Level	Age Level	Players	WHERE? Indoor	Out
Are You Out There?	2	B CD	8 +	I	O
Bell Bluff	2	B CD	6 +	I	
Blind Man's Bluff	2	B CD	6 +	I	O
Button Sort	2	B C	3 +	I	
Capture	2	B C	8 +	I	O
Cat and Dog	2	B CD	2 +	I	
Coin Collector	1	B CD	4 +	I	
Dark Draw	2	B	3 +	I	
Draw the Tail on the Donkey	2	B CD	3 +	I	
Fabric Match	1	AB	2 +	I	O
Pin the Tail on the Donkey	2	AB CD	3 +	I	
Pinch Me	3	B CD	10 +	I	
Share the Treat	1	B CD	4 +	I	O

CIRCLE GAMES (Participants Join to Form a Ring)

Title	Activity Level	Age Level	Players	WHERE? Indoor	Out
Air, Land, Water	1	B C	5 +	I	O
Are You Out There?	2	B CD	8 +	I	O
Ball Roll	2	A	3 +	I	O
Blind Man's Bluff	2	B CD	6 +	I	O
Bottle Answer	1	B CD	5 +	I	
Call Out Ball	3	B C	6 +		O
Capture	2	B C	8 +	I	O
Cat and Mouse	3	B C	10 +	I	O
Catch Ball	3	B C	10 +		O
Charley Over the Water	3	AB	6 +	I	O
Circle Race	3	AB C	3 +		O
Contrary Actions	2	B CD	4 +	I	O
Cooperative Tale	1	B CD	4 +	I	O

Title	Activity Level	Age Level	Players	Indoor	Out
Drop the Handkerchief	3	AB C	6 +	I	O
Duck, Duck, Gray Duck	3	AB	4 +	I	O
Farmer in the Dell	2	AB	8 +	I	O
Good Morning!	2	B C	6 +	I	O
Guess Ball	2	B C	4 +	I	O
Guess the Leader	2	B CD	6 +	I	
Ha, Ha, Ha	1	B CD	5 +	I	O
Hat Exchange	2	B CD	6 +	I	
Have You Seen My Friend?	3	B C	6 +	I	O
Holiday	1	B C	6 +	I	
Hot Money	2	AB C	8 +	I	O
Hot Potato	2	B CD	5 +	I	O
How Do You Like Your Neighbors?	2	B CD	5 +	I	O
Howdy, Neighbor	2	B CD	10 +		O
Kerchief Grab	3	B C	6 +	I	
Kerchief Relay	3	B	10 +	I	O
Laughing	2	AB CD	5 +	I	O
Pass the Prize	2	AB	5 +	I	O
People Puzzle	2	B CD	6 +	I	O
Poor Pussy	2	AB C	6 +	I	O
Progressive Story	1	CD	8 +	I	
Ring-Around-the-Rosy	2	A	3 +	I	O
Ring on a String	2	B CD	6 +	I	O
Spellout	1	B C	6 +	I	
What Animal Am I?	2	AB	4 +	I	

DRAWING AND PAINTING GAMES OR ACTIVITIES

Title	Activity Level	Age Level	Players	Indoor	Out
Artists	2	B CD	4 +	I	
Cooperative Art	2	AB C	4 +	I	
Dark Draw	2	B	3 +	I	
Dot Art	2	B CD	3 +	I	
Draw the Tail on the Donkey	2	B CD	3 +	I	
Making Squares	1	B CD	2 +	I	
Picture This	2	CD	6 +	I	

ELIMINATION GAMES ("Last Survivor" Wins)

Title	Activity Level	Age Level	Players	Indoor	Out
Alphabet Adjectives	1	B CD	4 +	I	
Balancing the Books	2	B C	3 +	I	
Balloon Break	3	B CD	4 +	I	O
Chain Tag	3	AB C	4 +		O
Circle Race	3	AB C	3 +		O

Contrary Actions	2	B CD	4 +	I	O
Fish	3	B CD	4 +	I	O
Grandmother's Trunk	1	B CD	3 +	I	O
Groups	2	B C	10 +	I	O
Ha, Ha, Ha	1	B CD	5 +	I	O
Hot Money	2	AB C	8 +	I	O
Hot Potato	2	B CD	5 +	I	O
Hunters and Hunted	3	B C	8 +	I	O
Mrs. O'Leary's Cow	1	B CD	3 +	I	
Musical Chairs	3	B CD	5 +	I	
Packing for a Trip	1	B CD	6 +	I	O
Pom Pom Pullaway	3	AB	3 +		O
Red Rover	3	B CD	8 +		O

GUESSING GAMES

Title	Activity Level	Age Level	Players	Indoor	WHERE? Out
Adverbs	1	D	4 +	I	
Advertisements	1	CD	5 +	I	O
Are You Out There?	2	B CD	8 +	I	O
Blind Man's Bluff	2	B CD	6 +	I	O
Colors	1	A	2 +	I	
Compliments	1	B CD	4 +	I	
Draw the Tail on the Donkey	2	B CD	3 +	I	
Forbidden Word	1	B CD	4 +	I	
Good Morning!	2	B C	6 +	I	O
Group Hide and Seek	2	AB	4 +	I	O
Guess Ball	2	B C	4 +	I	O
Guess the Leader	2	B CD	6 +	I	
Guessing Contest	1	B CD	4 +	I	O
Hangman	1	B CD	2 +	I	
Have You Seen My Friend?	3	B C	6 +	I	O
Hide and Seek	2	AB	4 +	I	O
Hot and Cold	2	AB	2 +	I	
Hunt the Thimble	2	B CD	4 +	I	
In This House	1	B C	3 +	I	
Letter Trace	1	AB	2 +	I	O
Murder	2	CD	6 +	I	
Paper, Scissors, Stone	2	B C	2 +	I	O
Picture This	2	CD	6 +	I	
Pin the Tail on the Donkey	2	AB CD	3 +	I	
Ring on a String	2	B CD	6 +	I	O
Sardines	2	B CD	4 +	I	
Sounds Like	1	B CD	3 +	I	
Toy Shop	2	AB	5 +	I	O
Treasure Hunt	2	B CD	6 +	I	O
Twenty Questions	1	B CD	5 +	I	
Up, Jenkins!	2	B CD	6 +	I	O

Title	Activity Level	Age Level	Players	Indoor	Out
Walking Game	2	B C D	2 +		O
What Am I Doing?	2	C D	8 +	I	
What Animal Am I?	2	A B	4 +	I	
What Word?	1	B C D	3 +	I	
Where Am I?	1	B C D	4 +	I	
Who Am I?	2	C D	4 +	I	O

"INSTANT" GAMES (No Special Preparations Are Required)

Title	Activity Level	Age Level	Players	WHERE? Indoor	WHERE? Out
Adverbs	1	D	4 +	I	
Affinities	1	C D	4 +	I	
Air, Land, Water	1	B C	5 +	I	O
Alphabet Adjectives	1	B C D	4 +	I	
Arise	2	B C	2 +	I	O
Arise for Two	2	B C	6 +	I	O
At Sea	3	B C D	8 +	I	O
Bird, Beast or Fish	1	B C D	6 +	I	O
Birds Fly	2	A B	3 +	I	O
Captain, May I?	2	B	5 +	I	O
Cat and Mouse	3	B C	10 +	I	O
Categories	1	C D	3 +	I	
Cause and Effect	1	B C D	3 +	I	
Chain Tag	3	A B C	4 +		O
Change Partners	2	B C	7 +	I	O
Charley Over the Water	3	A B	6 +	I	O
Colors	1	A	2 +	I	
Compliments	1	B C D	4 +	I	
Cooperative Tale	1	B C D	4 +	I	O
Dot Art	2	B C D	3 +	I	
Double Words	1	D	2 +	I	
Dramatic Poetry	1	B C D	4 +	I	
Duck, Duck, Gray Duck	3	A B	4 +	I	O
Famous Names	1	B C D	4 +	I	
Farmer in the Dell	2	A B	8 +	I	O
Follow the Leader	3	A B C D	4 +	I	O
Food for Thought	1	A B	2 +	I	O
Forbidden Word	1	B C D	4 +	I	
Good Morning!	2	B C	6 +	I	O
Grandmother's Trunk	1	B C D	3 +	I	O
Group Hide and Seek	2	A B	4 +	I	O
Groups	2	B C	10 +	I	O
Guess the Leader	2	B C D	6 +	I	
Ha, Ha, Ha	1	B C D	5 +	I	O
Hangman	1	B C D	2 +	I	
Have You Seen My Friend?	3	B C	6 +	I	O
Hide and Seek	2	A B	4 +	I	O
Holiday	1	B C	6 +	I	
Howdy, Neighbor	2	B C D	10 +		O

	Activity Level	Age Level	Players	Indoor	Out
Hunters and Hunted	3	B C	8 +	I	O
I Don't Like...	1	CD	4 +	I	
I Love My Love	1	CD	4 +	I	
In This House	1	B C	3 +	I	
Letter Trace	1	AB	2 +	I	O
London Bridge	2	A	4 +	I	O
Making Squares	1	B CD	2 +	I	
Mrs. O'Leary's Cow	1	B CD	3 +	I	
Nursery Rhyme	1	B	2 +	I	
Packing for a Trip	1	B CD	6 +	I	O
Pair Tag	3	B C	6 +		O
Paper, Scissors, Stone	2	B C	2 +	I	O
People Puzzle	2	B CD	6 +	I	O
Poor Pussy	2	AB C	6 +	I	O
Posing	2	B CD	6 +	I	O
Progressive Story	1	CD	8 +	I	
Pussy Wants a Corner	2	B	5 +	I	
Red Rover	3	B CD	8 +		O
Ring-Around-the-Rosy	2	A	3 +	I	O
Sardines	2	B CD	4 +	I	
Sculptor	2	B CD	5 +	I	O
Sensible Sentence	1	B CD	2 +	I	
Shadow Tag	3	B C	4 +		O
Shoe Scramble	3	A	3 +	I	O
Simon Says	3	AB C	4 +	I	O
Spellout	1	B C	6 +	I	
Squat Tag	3	AB C	4 +		O
Squirrel in a Tree	3	B CD	8 +	I	O
Statues	2	B CD	4 +	I	O
Tag	3	AB	3 +		O
Things	1	CD	4 +	I	
Toy Shop	2	AB	5 +	I	O
Twenty Questions	1	B CD	5 +	I	
Walking Game	2	B CD	2 +		O
What Am I Doing?	2	CD	8 +	I	
What Word?	1	B CD	3 +	I	
Where Am I?	1	B CD	4 +	I	
You've Got a...	1	B CD	3 +	I	

INTRODUCTORY, ICEBREAKER AND "MIXER" GAMES

Title	Activity Level	Age Level	Players	WHERE? Indoor	Out
Barnyard Buddy	2	B C	8 +	I	O
Change Partners	2	B C	7 +	I	O
Duet	2	B CD	6 +	I	O
Groups	2	B C	10 +	I	O
People Puzzle	2	B CD	6 +	I	O
Props	1	D	8 +	I	
Sing Along	2	B CD	10 +	I	O
"10"	2	B CD	10 +	I	O

Treasure Hunt	2	B C D	6 +	I	O
Word Match I	2	B C D	6 +	I	O
Word Match II	2	C D	10 +	I	O

MEMORY EXERCISES

Title	Activity Level	Age Level	Players	Indoor	WHERE? Out
Air, Land, Water	1	B C	5 +	I	O
Alphabet Adjectives	1	B C D	4 +	I	
Bird, Beast or Fish	1	B C D	6 +	I	O
Cooperative Tale	1	B C D	4 +	I	O
Dramatic Poetry	1	B C D	4 +	I	
Famous Names	1	B C D	4 +	I	
Grandmother's Trunk	1	B C D	3 +	I	O
In Plain Sight	2	C D	4 +	I	
Look and Remember	1	B C	3 +	I	O
Mrs. O'Leary's Cow	1	B C D	3 +	I	
Nursery Rhyme	1	B	2 +	I	
Packing for a Trip	1	B C D	6 +	I	O

MENTAL CONDITIONING (Invention, Concentration, Reasoning, etc.)

Title	Activity Level	Age Level	Players	Indoor	WHERE? Out
Adverbs	1	D	4 +	I	
Advertisements	1	C D	5 +	I	O
Affinities	1	C D	4 +	I	
Air, Land, Water	1	B C	5 +	I	O
Alphabet Adjectives	1	B C D	4 +	I	
Bird, Beast or Fish	1	B C D	6 +	I	O
Birds Fly	2	A B	3 +	I	O
Captain, May I?	2	B	5 +	I	O
Categories	1	C D	3 +	I	
Cause and Effect	1	B C D	3 +	I	
Celebrities	2	B C	4 +	I	
Chain Words	2	B C D	5 +	I	O
Contrary Actions	2	B C D	4 +	I	O
Cooperative Tale	1	B C D	4 +	I	O
Dark Draw	2	B	3 +	I	
Dot Art	2	B C D	3 +	I	
Double Words	1	D	2 +	I	
Famous Names	1	B C D	4 +	I	
Forbidden Word	1	B C D	4 +	I	
Grandmother's Trunk	1	B C D	3 +	I	O
Guess the Leader	2	B C D	6 +	I	
Ha, Ha, Ha	1	B C D	5 +	I	O
Hangman	1	B C D	2 +	I	
Holiday	1	B C	6 +	I	
I Don't Like...	1	C D	4 +	I	

I Love My Love	1	C D	4 +	I
In This House	1	B C	3 +	I
Laughing	2	AB C D	5 +	I O
Making Squares	1	B C D	2 +	I
Mrs. O'Leary's Cow	1	B C D	3 +	I
Murder	2	C D	6 +	I
Packing for a Trip	1	B C D	6 +	I O
Paper, Scissors, Stone	2	B C	2 +	I O
Picture This	2	C D	6 +	I
Props	1	D	8 +	I
Sculptor	2	B C D	5 +	I O
Sensible Sentence	1	B C D	2 +	I
Simon Says	3	AB C	4 +	I O
Spellout	1	B C	6 +	I
Statues	2	B C D	4 +	I O
Things	1	C D	4 +	I
Treasure Hunt	2	B C D	6 +	I O
Twenty Questions	1	B C D	5 +	I
Where Am I?	1	B C D	4 +	I
Who Am I?	2	C D	4 +	I O
Yes and No	1	B C D	3 +	I O
You've Got a...	1	B C D	3 +	I

MIMICRY, PANTOMIME

Title	Activity Level	Age Level	Players	WHERE? Indoor	Out
Adverbs	1	D	4 +	I	
Are You Out There?	2	B C D	8 +	I	O
Barnyard Buddy	2	B C	8 +	I	O
Celebrities	2	B C	4 +	I	
Dramatic Poetry	1	B C D	4 +	I	
Follow the Leader	3	AB C D	4 +	I	O
Guess the Leader	2	B C D	6 +	I	
Poor Pussy	2	AB C	6 +	I	O
Posing	2	B C D	6 +	I	O
Props	1	D	8 +	I	
Puppy Race	3	AB	4 +		O
Toy Shop	2	AB	5 +	I	O
What Am I Doing?	2	C D	8 +	I	
What Animal Am I?	2	AB	4 +	I	

MUSICAL GAMES, NONSINGING

Title	Activity Level	Age Level	Players	WHERE? Indoor	Out
Are You Out There?	2	B C D	8 +	I	O
Group Musical Chairs	3	AB	4 +	I	O
Hot Money	2	AB C	8 +	I	O
Hot Potato	2	B C D	5 +	I	O

Musical Chairs	3	B CD	5 +	I	
Pass the Prize	2	AB	5 +	I	O

MUSICAL GAMES, SINGING

Title	Activity Level	Age Level	Players	WHERE? Indoor	Out
Charley Over the Water	3	AB	6 +	I	O
Duet	2	B CD	6 +	I	O
Farmer in the Dell	2	AB	8 +	I	O
Find It	2	B CD	6 +	I	
Hunt the Thimble	2	B CD	4 +	I	
London Bridge	2	A	4 +	I	O
Ring-Around-the-Rosy	2	A	3 +	I	O
Sing Along	2	B CD	10 +	I	O

MYSTERY OR SURPRISE

Title	Activity Level	Age Level	Players	WHERE? Indoor	Out
Are You Out There?	2	B CD	8 +	I	O
Barnyard Buddy	2	B C	8 +	I	O
Blind Man's Bluff	2	B CD	6 +	I	O
Bottle Answer	1	B CD	5 +	I	
Capture	2	B C	8 +	I	O
Cat and Dog	2	B CD	2 +	I	
Dark Draw	2	B	3 +	I	
Draw the Tail on the Donkey	2	B CD	3 +	I	
Find It	2	B CD	6 +	I	
Good Morning!	2	B C	6 +	I	O
Group Hide and Seek	2	AB	4 +	I	O
Hangman	1	B CD	2 +	I	
Hide and Seek	2	AB	4 +	I	O
Hot and Cold	2	AB	2 +	I	
Murder	2	CD	6 +	I	
Pin the Tail on the Donkey	2	AB CD	3 +	I	
Pinch Me	3	B CD	10 +	I	
Progressive Story	1	CD	8 +	I	
Sardines	2	B CD	4 +	I	
Share the Treat	1	B CD	4 +	I	O
Spider Web	2	AB	2 +	I	O
Treasure Hunt	2	B CD	6 +	I	O
Twenty Questions	1	B CD	5 +	I	

PHYSICAL CONDITIONING (Agility, Balance, Coordination, Endurance)

Title	Activity Level	Age Level	Players	WHERE? Indoor	Out
Airplane Race	2	AB C	6 +	I	O
Amoeba	3	B CD	6 +		O
Arise	2	B C	2 +	I	O
Arise for Two	2	B C	6 +	I	O
Backward Bowling	2	B C	2 +		O
Balancing the Books	2	B C	3 +	I	
Ball Roll	2	A	3 +	I	O
Balloon Ball	3	B C	8 +	I	
Balloon Break	3	B CD	4 +	I	O
Balloon Relay	3	B CD	6 +	I	O
Balloon Volleyball	3	B CD	4 +		O
Bean Transfer	2	B C	6 +	I	
Bell Bluff	2	B CD	6 +	I	
Bellringer	2	AB	4 +		O
Bounce	2	B C	2 +	I	O
Call Ball	3	B C	4 +		O
Call Out Ball	3	B C	6 +		O
Captain, May I?	2	B	5 +	I	O
Capture	2	B C	8 +	I	O
Capture the Flag	3	B	6 +	I	O
Cat and Dog	2	B CD	2 +	I	
Cat and Mice	3	B	8 +		O
Cat and Mouse	3	B C	10 +	I	O
Catch Ball	3	B C	10 +		O
Caterpillar Race	3	B C	8 +		O
Chain Tag	3	AB C	4 +		O
Chin Game	2	CD	8 +	I	O
Circle Race	3	AB C	3 +		O
Circle Tug of War	3	B CD	8 +		O
Coat and Hat Relay	3	B C	8 +		O
Coin Drop	1	AB	2 +	I	
Contrary Actions	2	B CD	4 +	I	O
Drop the Handkerchief	3	AB C	6 +	I	O
Duck, Duck, Gray Duck	3	AB	4 +	I	O
Duck Walk	3	B	2 +	I	O
Egg Race	2	B CD	4 +	I	O
Feather Float	3	B CD	8 +	I	O
Fish	3	B CD	4 +	I	O
Fishing for Paper Clips	2	AB C	2 +	I	
Follow the Leader	3	AB CD	4 +	I	O
Glove Relay	2	B CD	6 +	I	
Group Musical Chairs	3	AB	4 +	I	O
Hat Exchange	2	B CD	6 +	I	
Have You Seen My Friend?	3	B C	6 +	I	O
How Do You Like Your Neighbors?	2	B CD	5 +	I	O
Howdy, Neighbor	2	B CD	10 +		O

125

Title	Activity Level	Age Level	Players	Indoor	Out
Hunters and Hunted	3	B C	8 +	I	O
Indoor Football	2	AB CD	4 +	I	
Kangaroo Race	3	B C	3 +	I	O
Keep Away	3	B C	3 +		O
Kerchief Grab	3	B C	6 +	I	
Kerchief Relay	3	B	10 +	I	O
Lifesaver Relay	2	B CD	8 +	I	
Marble Golf	2	B C	3 +		O
Musical Chairs	3	B CD	5 +	I	
Pair Tag	3	B C	6 +		O
Peanut Drop	1	B CD	3 +	I	
Peanut Relay	2	B CD	6 +	I	O
Pickle in the Middle	3	B	3	I	O
Pitch and Catch	3	B	8 +		O
Plate Sailing	2	B CD	2 +	I	O
Pom Pom Pullaway	3	AB	3 +		O
Puppy Race	3	AB	4 +		O
Red Rover	3	B CD	8 +		O
Ribbon Cutting	2	B CD	4 +	I	
Ring Relay	2	B CD	8 +	I	
Sculptor	2	B CD	5 +	I	O
Shadow Tag	3	B C	4 +		O
Shoe Match	2	A	5 +	I	
Shoe Put	3	B CD	3 +		O
Simon Says	3	AB C	4 +	I	O
Squat Tag	3	AB C	4 +		O
Squirrel in a Tree	3	B CD	8 +	I	O
Statues	2	B CD	4 +	I	O
Suitcase Relay	3	B CD	8 +	I	O
Tag	3	AB	3 +		O
Umbrella Ball	2	B CD	2 +	I	
Wastebasket Ball	1	B CD	3 +	I	

PRIZES AWARDED TO WINNER(S)

Title	Activity Level	Age Level	Players	WHERE? Indoor	Out
Affinities	1	CD	4 +	I	
Bounce	2	B C	2 +	I	O
Coin Drop	1	AB	2 +	I	
Find It	2	B CD	6 +	I	
Guessing Contest	1	B CD	4 +	I	O
Hot and Cold	2	AB	2 +	I	
Pass the Prize	2	AB	5 +	I	O
Spider Web	2	AB	2 +	I	O
"10"	2	B CD	10 +	I	O
Treasure Hunt	2	B CD	6 +	I	O

Index to Games by Type

QUIET GAMES

Title	Activity Level	Age Level	Players	WHERE? Indoor	Out
Affinities	1	CD	4 +	I	
Alphabet Adjectives	1	B C D	4 +	I	
Birds Fly	2	AB	3 +	I	O
Bounce	2	B C	2 +	I	O
Button Sort	2	B C	3 +	I	
Card Toss	1	B C	4 +	I	
Categories	1	CD	3 +	I	
Cause and Effect	1	B C D	3 +	I	
Celebrities	2	B C	4 +	I	
Chain Words	2	B C D	5 +	I	O
Coin Collector	1	B C D	4 +	I	
Coin Drop	1	AB	2 +	I	
Colors	1	A	2 +	I	
Compliments	1	B C D	4 +	I	
Cooperative Art	2	AB C	4 +	I	
Cooperative Tale	1	B C D	4 +	I	O
Dark Draw	2	B	3 +	I	
Dot Art	2	B C D	3 +	I	
Double Words	1	D	2 +	I	
Fabric Match	1	AB	2 +	I	O
Famous Names	1	B C D	4 +	I	
Fishing for Paper Clips	2	AB C	2 +	I	
Grandmother's Trunk	1	B C D	3 +	I	O
Guessing Contest	1	B C D	4 +	I	O
Hangman	1	B C D	2 +	I	
I Don't Like...	1	CD	4 +	I	
I Love My Love	1	CD	4 +	I	
In Plain Sight	2	CD	4 +	I	
In This House	1	B C	3 +	I	
Letter Trace	1	AB	2 +	I	O
Look and Remember	1	B C	3 +	I	O
Making Squares	1	B C D	2 +	I	
Mrs. O'Leary's Cow	1	B C D	3 +	I	
Nursery Rhyme	1	B	2 +	I	
Packing for a Trip	1	B C D	6 +	I	O
Paper, Scissors, Stone	2	B C	2 +	I	O
Peanut Drop	1	B C D	3 +	I	
Picture This	2	CD	6 +	I	
Plate Sailing	2	B C D	2 +	I	O
Progressive Story	1	CD	8 +	I	
Sensible Sentence	1	B C D	2 +	I	
Spellout	1	B C	6 +	I	
Things	1	CD	4 +	I	
Twenty Questions	1	B C D	5 +	I	
What Word?	1	B C D	3 +	I	
Where Am I?	1	B C D	4 +	I	
You've Got a...	1	B C D	3 +	I	

RACES, NONRUNNING

Title	Activity Level	Age Level	Players	Indoor	Out
Airplane Race	2	AB C	6 +	I	O
Amoeba	3	B CD	6 +		O
Arise for Two	2	B C	6 +	I	O
Bean Transfer	2	B C	6 +	I	
Button Sort	2	B C	3 +	I	
Chin Game	2	CD	8 +	I	O
Coin Collector	1	B CD	4 +	I	
Duck Walk	3	B	2 +	I	O
Egg Race	2	B CD	4 +	I	O
Famous Names	1	B CD	4 +	I	
Feather Float	3	B CD	8 +	I	O
Glove Relay	2	B CD	6 +	I	
Indoor Football	2	AB CD	4 +	I	
Kangaroo Race	3	B C	3 +	I	O
Kerchief Relay	3	B	10 +	I	O
Lifesaver Relay	2	B CD	8 +	I	
Pass It On	2	AB C	6 +	I	O
Peanut Drop	1	B CD	3 +	I	
Peanut Relay	2	B CD	6 +	I	O
Puppy Race	3	AB	4 +		O
Pussy Wants a Corner	2	B	5 +	I	
Ribbon Cutting	2	B CD	4 +	I	
Ring Relay	2	B CD	8 +	I	
Share the Treat	1	B CD	4 +	I	O
Shoe Scramble	3	A	3 +	I	O
Statues	2	B CD	4 +	I	O
Things	1	CD	4 +	I	

RELAY GAMES

Title	Activity Level	Age Level	Players	Indoor	Out
Balloon Relay	3	B CD	6 +	I	O
Chin Game	2	CD	8 +	I	O
Coat and Hat Relay	3	B C	8 +		O
Glove Relay	2	B CD	6 +	I	
Kerchief Relay	3	B	10 +	I	O
Lifesaver Relay	2	B CD	8 +	I	
Pass It On	2	AB C	6 +	I	O
Peanut Relay	2	B CD	6 +	I	O
Pitch and Catch	3	B	8 +		O
Ring Relay	2	B CD	8 +	I	
String Relay	2	B C	6 +	I	O
Suitcase Relay	3	B CD	8 +	I	O

RUNNING GAMES

Title	Activity Level	Age Level	Players	Indoor	Out
At Sea	3	B C D	8 +	I	O
Balloon Relay	3	B C D	6 +	I	O
Call Out Ball	3	B C	6 +		O
Capture the Flag	3	B	6 +	I	O
Cat and Mice	3	B	8 +		O
Caterpillar Race	3	B C	8 +		O
Chain Tag	3	A B C	4 +		O
Circle Race	3	A B C	3 +		O
Coat and Hat Relay	3	B C	8 +		O
Drop the Handkerchief	3	A B C	6 +	I	O
Duck, Duck, Gray Duck	3	A B	4 +	I	O
Fire Chief	3	B C	13 +		O
Go Find the Swatter	3	B	5 +	I	O
Have You Seen My Friend?	3	B C	6 +	I	O
Howdy, Neighbor	2	B C D	10 +		O
Kerchief Grab	3	B C	6 +	I	
Pair Tag	3	B C	6 +		O
Pitch and Catch	3	B	8 +		O
Pom Pom Pullaway	3	A B	3 +		O
Red Rover	3	B C D	8 +		O
Shadow Tag	3	B C	4 +		O
Shoe Scramble	3	A	3 +	I	O
Squat Tag	3	A B C	4 +		O
Tag	3	A B	3 +		O

SENSORY CONDITIONING (Tactile Skills)

Title	Activity Level	Age Level	Players	Indoor	Out
Blind Man's Bluff	2	B C D	6 +	I	O
Button Sort	2	B C	3 +	I	
Coin Collector	1	B C D	4 +	I	
Dark Draw	2	B	3 +	I	
Fabric Match	1	A B	2 +	I	O
Letter Trace	1	A B	2 +	I	O

TAG GAMES

Title	Activity Level	Age Level	Players	Indoor	Out
Bell Bluff	2	B C D	6 +	I	
Capture	2	B C	8 +	I	O
Cat and Dog	2	B C D	2 +	I	
Cat and Mice	3	B	8 +		O
Cat and Mouse	3	B C	10 +	I	O

Chain Tag	3	AB C	4 +		O
Charley Over the Water	3	AB	6 +	I	O
Circle Race	3	AB C	3 +		O
Drop the Handkerchief	3	AB C	6 +	I	O
Duck, Duck, Gray Duck	3	AB	4 +	I	O
Fire Chief	3	B C	13 +		O
Go Find the Swatter	3	B	5 +	I	O
Have You Seen My Friend?	3	B C	6 +	I	O
Pair Tag	3	B C	6 +		O
Pom Pom Pullaway	3	AB	3 +		O
Shadow Tag	3	B C	4 +		O
Squat Tag	3	AB C	4 +		O
Tag	3	AB	3 +		O

TEAM GAMES

Title	Activity Level	Age Level	Players	Indoor	Out
Airplane Race	2	AB C	6 +	I	O
Amoeba	3	B CD	6 +		O
Arise for Two	2	B C	6 +	I	O
Balloon Ball	3	B C	8 +	I	
Balloon Relay	3	B CD	6 +	I	O
Balloon Volleyball	3	B CD	4 +		O
Bean Transfer	2	B C	6 +	I	
Capture the Flag	3	B	6 +	I	O
Card Toss	1	B C	4 +	I	
Caterpillar Race	3	B C	8 +		O
Chin Game	2	CD	8 +	I	O
Circle Tug of War	3	B CD	8 +		O
Coat and Hat Relay	3	B C	8 +		O
Feather Float	3	B CD	8 +	I	O
Glove Relay	2	B CD	6 +	I	
Hunters and Hunted	3	B C	8 +	I	O
In Plain Sight	2	CD	4 +	I	
Indoor Football	2	AB CD	4 +	I	
Indoor Scavenger Hunt	1	D	6 +	I	
Kerchief Relay	3	B	10 +	I	O
Lifesaver Relay	2	B CD	8 +	I	
Pass It On	2	AB C	6 +	I	O
Peanut Relay	2	B CD	6 +	I	O
Picture This	2	CD	6 +	I	
Pitch and Catch	3	B	8 +		O
Props	1	D	8 +	I	
Red Rover	3	B CD	8 +		O
Ribbon Cutting	2	B CD	4 +	I	
Ring Relay	2	B CD	8 +	I	
Scavenger Hunt	1	B CD	6 +		O
Share the Treat	1	B CD	4 +	I	O
String Relay	2	B C	6 +	I	O

				WHERE?	
				Indoor	Out
Suitcase Relay	3	B CD	8 +	I	O
Up, Jenkins!	2	B CD	6 +	I	O

THROWING OR TOSSING GAMES

Title	Activity Level	Age Level	Players	Indoor	Out
				WHERE?	
Backward Bowling	2	B C	2 +		O
Bellringer	2	AB	4 +		O
Call Ball	3	B C	4 +		O
Call Out Ball	3	B C	6 +		O
Card Toss	1	B C	4 +	I	
Catch Ball	3	B C	10 +		O
Chain Words	2	B CD	5 +	I	O
Guess Ball	2	B C	4 +	I	O
Keep Away	3	B C	3 +		O
Kerchief Grab	3	B C	6 +	I	
Laughing	2	AB CD	5 +	I	O
Pickle in the Middle	3	B	3	I	O
Pitch and Catch	3	B	8 +		O
Plate Sailing	2	B CD	2 +	I	O
Shoe Put	3	B CD	3 +		O

WORD GAMES

Title	Activity Level	Age Level	Players	Indoor	Out
				WHERE?	
Air, Land, Water	1	B C	5 +	I	O
Adverbs	1	D	4 +	I	
Affinities	1	CD	4 +	I	
Alphabet Adjectives	1	B CD	4 +	I	
Bird, Beast or Fish	1	B CD	6 +	I	O
Categories	1	CD	3 +	I	
Cause and Effect	1	B CD	3 +	I	
Chain Words	2	B CD	5 +	I	O
Cooperative Tale	1	B CD	4 +	I	O
Double Words	1	D	2 +	I	
Famous Names	1	B CD	4 +	I	
Food for Thought	1	AB	2 +	I	O
Forbidden Word	1	B CD	4 +	I	
Hangman	1	B CD	2 +	I	
Holiday	1	B C	6 +	I	
I Don't Like...	1	CD	4 +	I	
I Love My Love	1	CD	4 +	I	
Mrs. O'Leary's Cow	1	B CD	3 +	I	
Nursery Rhyme	1	B	2 +	I	
Packing for a Trip	1	B CD	6 +	I	O
Picture This	2	CD	6 +	I	
Progressive Story	1	CD	8 +	I	
Sensible Sentence	1	B CD	2 +	I	

Spellout	1	B C	6 +	I	
Things	1	CD	4 +	I	
Twenty Questions	1	B CD	5 +	I	
What Word?	1	B CD	3 +	I	
Word Match I	2	B CD	6 +	I	O
Word Match II	2	CD	10 +	I	O
You've Got a...	1	B CD	3 +	I	

Bibliography

Arnold, Arnold, **World Book of Children's Games,** World, 1972.

Beaver, Patrick, **Victorian Parlor Games,** Thomas Nelson, Inc., 1974.

Boehm, David Alfred, **The Family Game Book,** Doubleday & Co., 1967.

Brent, Ruth, **Ruth Brent's Book of Parties for the Bride,** McGraw Hill, 1959.

Burns, Lorell Coffman, **Instant Party Fun,** Association Press, 1967.

Cleaver, Nancy, **Treasury of Family Fun,** Revell, 1960.

Dennison Complete Party Guide, Dennison Manufacturing Co., 1961.

Depew, Arthur M., **Cokesbury Party Book,** Abingdon, 1959.

Donnelly, Richard F.; Helms, William G. and Mitchell, Elmer D., **Active Games and Contests,** Ronald Press, 1958.

Dubber, Patricia, **The Party Book (Service Book #126),** Educational Research Bureau, 1946.

Eisenberg, Helen & Larry, **Family Fun Book,** Association Press, 1953.

Eisenberg, Helen & Larry, **Handbook of Skits and Stunts,** Association Press, 1953.

Eisenberg, Helen & Larry, **Omnibus of Fun,** Association Press, 1956.

Fixx, James F., **Games for the Superintelligent,** Doubleday, 1972.

Good Housekeeping Complete Book of Home Entertaining, Good Housekeeping Books, 1971.

Harbin, Elvin Oscar, **Fun Encyclopedia,** Abingdon Press, 1940.

Hartley, Ruth E. and Goldenson, Robert M., **Complete Book of Children's Play**, Crowell, 1963.

Highlights Handbook of Party Plans, Highlights for Children, Inc., 1959.

Hindman, Darwin Alexander, **Complete Book of Games and Stunts**, Prentice-Hall, Inc., 1956.

Hogan, Bernice, **Fun Party Games**, Hewitt House, 1969.

Hopkins, Ginny, **The Bride's Book of Showers**, Grosset & Dunlap, 1971.

Ickis, Marguerite, **Book of Games and Entertainment the World Over**, Dodd Mead, 1969.

Ilg, Frances, **Gesell Institute Party Book**, Harper, 1959.

Kemmerer, James W. and Brickett, Eva May, **Games and Parties for All Occasions**, Baker Book House, 1962.

Kraus, Richard G., **Family Book of Games**, McGraw, 1960.

McFarlan, Allan A., **More New Games for 'Tween-Agers**, Association Press, 1958.

Mulac, Margaret E., **Fun and Games**, Harper & Row, 1956.

Mulac, Margaret E., **Games and Stunts for Schools, Camps and Playgrounds**, Harper & Row, 1964.

Musselman, Virginia, **Instant Picnic Fun**, Association Press, 1967.

Musselman, Virginia, **Making Children's Parties Click**, Stackpole Books, 1967.

Musselman, Virginia, **Making Family Get-Togethers Click**, Stackpole Books, 1968.

Orlick, Terry, **Cooperative Sports and Games Book**, Pantheon, 1978.

Rice, Wayne; Rydberg, Denny and Yaconelli, Mike, **Fun 'n' Games**, Zondervan Publishing, 1977.

Bibliography

Stein, Lincoln David, **Family Games,** MacMillan, 1979.

Sternlicht, Manny, **Games Children Play: Instructive and Creative Play Activities for the Mentally Retarded and Developmentally Disabled Child,** Van Nostrand, 1981.

Strobell, Adah Parker, **"Like it Was" Bicentennial Games 'N Fun Handbook,** Acropolis Books, Ltd., 1975.

Thomas, Robert, **Games, Any One?,** Doubleday, 1964.

Van Rensselaer, Alexander, **Complete Book of Party Games,** Sheridan House, 1952.

Vinton, Iris, **Folkways Omnibus of Children's Games,** Hawthorn Books, 1970.

Wolfsohn, Reeta Bochner, **Successful Children's Parties,** Arco, 1979.